FACING HARD TIMES AND GOOD TIMES WITH GRATITUDE

MW01127332

LARRY RICE

©2022 Larry Rice, New Life Evangelistic Center. All Rights Reserved. New Life Evangelistic Center, 2428 Woodson Rd. Overland, MO 63114. www.nlecstl.org

Contents

Chapter 1
Hearts on Fire for Jesus

The year 2022 is the year that New Life Evangelistic Center is celebrating fifty years of God's faithfulness. This faithfulness is evident through the countless times our Heavenly Father miraculously transformed the lives of the hurting and homeless as He provided both the finances and the NLEC team members to carry out His work. When a legal lynching resulted in the closing of 1411 Locust headquarters in April 2017, God was there. In the years following, the Holy Spirit continued to open new doors of opportunity for New Life Evangelistic Center to directly help the poor and homeless as it shared the good news of Christ resurrection.

First Edition – ZOA Free Paper, January 1973

New Life Evangelistic Center was founded in January 1972 in a fifty-foot trailer where Penny and I lived in Wellston, Missouri. From the time it began NLEC was a total faith ministry which depended on God to provide. I wrote at that time, "The future does look uncertain. New Life has no financial backing from any church or denomination. All I have is a deep desire to serve God and start a work that will glorify him in word and in deed."

It was the fact that we knew Christ was risen and the power of the Holy Spirit was at work that we shared the hope of the resurrection with everyone everywhere. With hearts on fire for Jesus, we would work all night finishing our witnessing tool called the New Life ZOA Free Paper. It was filled with testimonies of people whose lives had been changed through the love of Christ. Those testimonies included NLEC student Sandy Luebke who reported, "Three years ago I was hospitalized, after a near fatal suicide attempt. My mother was told by doctors that I was acutely and hopelessly depressed, and because my only ambition was to take my life, that I'd have to be in institutions the rest of my life. Then I said "Yes" to God by giving my life to Christ. He totally transformed my life, giving me a peace and love I had never known. Along with this love He gave me a new purpose for living by bringing me to New Life Evangelistic

Center."

With hearts aflame and the assurance of God's presence and love, Penny and I would open our homes all hours of the night to the homeless and hurting. To those who had given up on government, the church, and the family we would witness to the fact that there was hope because Christ was risen. Ray Davis was one of our housing guests who experienced the life changing power of Jesus Christ. He shared his testimony in the ZOA Paper. "My search for love was a frustrating experience which thrust me into 20 years of alcoholism. Finally, I said 'Yes' to God and received His love which was demonstrated through His Son, Jesus Christ. Now I have found not only love but peace, purpose, and hope as well."

Historians refer to the 1970's as the period when Americans finally had to accept that their political system had serious flaws. They had lost trust in their elected officials and even democracy itself. Many were willing to openly engage in conversations concerning the meaning for life and God's love for them.

In 2020 the State Historical Society in Missouri acquired from New Life Evangelistic Center it's records, correspon-

Training Disciples to Turn the World on to Jesus Christ!

dences, publications, videos etc. to keep on permanent record at its St. Louis Research Center for future generations. A.J. Maddock the director of that center wrote the following in February 2020 in the Missouri Times concerning the early years in the work of New Life Evangelistic Center.

"Among the newest collections available at the St. Louis Research Center are the papers of the New Life Evangelistic Center (NLEC). Established by minister Larry Rice in 1972, New Life emphasizes care for the poor by providing food and clothing, emergency shelter, job training programs, and spiritual care. Legal problems forced New Life to close its St. Louis shelter on 1411 Locust Street in 2017, but efforts are underway to reopen it. New Life continues to provide services through its administrative office in Overland, Missouri."

"The St. Louis center's NLEC records contain correspondence, meeting minutes, and photographs depicting the founding and expansion of NLEC's ministry from 1972 to 2018. Among the notable features in the collection are issues of the ZOA Free Paper, NLEC's in-house publication. The newspaper chronicles New Life's beginnings as an offshoot of the Jesus Movement, a religious movement that took hold among a segment of the nation's youth in the 1960's and 1970's. It had spawned coffeehouses, communes, and marches that echoed the countercultural movement of the 1960's."

"Rice fashioned the ZOA Free Paper after similar underground newspapers that had sprouted on the West Coast at that time, including the Hollywood Free Paper in Los Angeles. "Zoa" is the Greek word for life. In the first issue of the ZOA Free Paper, Rice editorialized that he wanted NLEC and its publication to encourage St. Louisans to reject the "establishment" in favor of seeking zoa (life in Jesus Christ)."

2107 Park Ave.

"An early advertisement in the ZOA Free Paper promoted NLEC's Catacombs Coffeehouse, built in an old coal tunnel under NLEC's original headquarters at 2107 Park Avenue in Lafayette Square. The coffeehouse was portrayed as a Saturday night hangout for children and teens, with one ad featuring a photograph of NLEC youths listening to a rock band. Up to that point, traditional Christian denominations had frowned on secular-sounding music. One of the major innovations of the Jesus Movement was to combine modern music with Christian lyrics, a form of worship now found in many churches."

"By the mid-1970s, the Jesus Movement, like the broader countercultural movement, was in decline, and many of the institutions it inspired began to fold. Rice's ministry proved to be a long-lived exception. As New Life seeks to reopen its facility in St. Louis, it continues to operate online and on low-powered television channels to communicate its message."

"The NLEC papers offer a valuable source of information on the Jesus Movement in St. Louis and ministry for the poor and homeless in Missouri. For more information on how to access this collection, contact the St. Louis Research Center at stlouis@shsmo.org."

In 1978 as the NLEC Staff continued to tell everyone we met that there is hope because Christ is risen, the Holy Spirit laid it on my heart that we had to do more than just talk the talk. We had to directly help the poor and homeless meet the daily needs they were facing. We discovered that direct financial grants to those facing the shut off of their utilities, gifts of blankets, space heaters, wood burning stoves, shelter, food, etc. gave us unprecedented

Sharing the love of Jesus with a man during Winter Street Patrol.

opportunities to share the love of Jesus Christ in both word and deed.

I had seen once we had done everything we could for that brother or sister in need we were free to go to God in intercessory prayer with a clear conscience saying, "Father, I have done everything I can in faith with the resources you have given me. Now I ask you in the name of Jesus Christ for your direct divine intervention in this situation." The result—IT WORKS! Miracles happen and the need is supplied!

First Board of Directors for

In Matt 25:40 Jesus said, "I tell you the truth, whatever you did for one of the least of these brothers [or sisters] of mine; you did for me". This verse further motivated me to help a man who was deaf. This homeless deaf man wrote out how he had arrived in St. Louis only to be robbed and then spent three nights sleeping outside until someone directed him to our shelter at 1411 Locust Street. I knew there were many others who were struggling outside and needed to be helped. After hearing of the winter patrol that was taking place in Washington D.C. I felt the Holy Spirit leading me to start one in St. Louis to find the homeless and bring them to shelter.

To accomplish this goal, men staying in our shelter were invited to ride with myself and other NLEC team members to help us find where the homeless were sleeping outside. When we found the homeless, we would invite them to come with us to receive shelter, food, blankets, and other assistance.

Ray Redlich and a Volunteer checking on homeless man sleeping outside 2012.

Ray Redlich was right beside me when winter patrol started in 1978 and continues to be there today. Ray shared his memories from those early years.

"It was a cold night in December 1978. Little did I know that as I went out with my trusted leader Rev. Larry Rice on a new venture call "winter patrol," that it would radically change my perspective on homelessness and would launch me into a new vocation of street outreach."

"Not that we weren't already working with the homeless. Since its inception, the New Life Evangelistic Center had always been directly involved—hands on—with persons who had nowhere to live, providing overnight shelter, food, and Christian compassion."

"But the winter patrol went a step further. Larry took me out that night to places where I had no idea human beings were living. In sub-zero weather we found people sleeping in abandoned buildings and on the porches of old houses. To my astonishment we even discovered a man outdoors wrapped in an old carpet! I must admit it opened a new world to me. From henceforth it wouldn't be enough just to wait for those in need to come to us. We would also have to go out and find them."

"Over 40 years have passed since my first exposure to winter patrol. I could recount a host of experiences—some frightening, some heart-warming, but all life-changing in the sense that they have given me a better understanding of my fellow human beings."

"One of the most encouraging aspects of the winter patrol has been the joy of seeing so many volunteers from all walks of life join alongside us. Most of them were not professional social workers or other specialists, but just ordinary caring individuals who wanted to make a difference, who were willing to step out of their comfort zones to help—and get to know—their fellow human beings. As a result, we have put a lot of people to work over the years (although it never seemed enough), and several groups have actually "spun off" to form outreach teams and even shelters of their own. It's great to know that our work can inspire others to find creative ways to help."

Homeless man living in a tunnel with his dog.

"We have had to learn and adapt as we faced new challenges. Several years ago, the city of St. Louis closed out principal homeless shelter in downtown St. Louis—a casualty of the growing nationwide conflict of gentrification versus traditional human services. That closure thrust me and several of my co-workers out on the streets more than ever before. If the homeless could no longer come to us, then we must go out to them—daytime and nighttime, all year long."

"It has proved a powerful education for me. Once again, I have come to see homelessness from a new perspective. We now go out daily to where the homeless live—on the street corners, under bridges, in abandoned houses and industrial buildings. We visit them in tent encampments. (Yes, the homeless often desire to dwell in mutually helpful communities, just like the rest of us.) Often, we come to know and love certain individuals, only to find out that they have died from violence, drug overdose or illness on the streets."

Homeless man sleeping on sidewalk.

"We always try to improve our outreach. COVID has presented unique challenges for homeless providers—both those offering shelter and those doing street outreach. Recently Joe Colonna, a NLEC volunteer has started a regular outreach in St. Louis County—the suburban area where there are virtually no services for the homeless."

"NLEC continues to reach out ... and to recruit others to join in the struggle. NLEC offers the homeless life-changing opportunities through the New Life Leadership Training Program, the Women's Safe Houses and other resources such as placement and transportation assistance. Yes, the struggle involves never-ending challenges, but also incredible joy as the homeless learn the love of Jesus Christ."

The opportunity to provide for the growing numbers of home-

NLEC Staff in
the early years

less women had been given to us through the opportunity to acquire 422 St. Louis Ave., in East St. Louis. This building had formerly been a boarding house, but now the lady owning it had offered it to us for the homeless. As we shared the need for this three-story facility, complete with a kitchen, staff quarters and individual rooms for the guests, we witnessed God provide the $12,000 we needed to acquire this building. Roberta Benjamin, a middle aged African American woman, and Judy Schlimpert, the very talented blind woman who was helping us acquire Channel 24, moved into the building on July 1, 1980. This was also the day that temperatures reached 103 degrees and thrust Mid America into one of the greatest heat crises in history.

As the heat continued to persist, the sick and elderly started dying. I would wake up hearing the ambulances race down Park Ave., all

Larry Rice showing woman the fan she is going to receive.

hours of the day and night. They were transporting the poor and elderly overcome by the heat to the Old City Hospital at 14th and Lafayette Ave. I began to pray, "Dear God please give us money for fans."

It was on July 10, when NLEC received a call from the mayor's office saying that an elderly woman from North St. Louis had

contacted them pleading for a fan. I responded to that call and proceeded to the address given. When I knocked on the door, I identified myself, and stated I had come with a fan. Suddenly the door flew open, and I heard seventy-six-year-old blind Ophelia Mack answer the door and cry out "Thank God! Now I know he loves me."

The next morning when I arrived at the office, I picked up a small envelope marked for my personal attention. In it was a note: 'Please use the enclosed for fans for the elderly'.

In the envelope was a check for $3,500. It was then I knew with certainty what must be done. We had to step out in faith and give 1,000 new fans to the elderly.

As we took God at His word when He said, "Try me now" (Malachi 3:10) and as we let the Holy Spirit work through us, we saw "Him do exceedingly more than we could ask or think" (Eph. 3:20). During the first thirteen years we saw God provide

Elderly woman with A/C unit.

New Life Evangelistic Center with two full powered television stations, tens of thousands of homeless people sheltered, the multitudes fed, given blankets, heaters, fans, and air conditioners. God through His faithfulness made it possible for NLEC to host major Thanksgiving and Christmas parties and much more.

Dr. Paul R. Ahr, the former director of Mental Health for the State of Missouri wrote in a letter to New Life Evangelistic Center, "In 1980 during the appropriations hearings, Rep. Bob Brandhorst of St. Louis asked me of my opinion of the New Life Evangelistic Center (NLEC) and Rev. Larry Rice. Repeating the little I had heard from professionals in the St. Louis area, I said that both warranted mixed reviews, with a tendency toward the unfavorable. Rep. Brandhorst was not pleased."

"Quickly realizing that I needed to form my own opinion of NLEC and you, I traveled to St. Louis where you graciously took me on "night patrol." I vividly recall how cold it was that night, often relating that if it had been that cold in Hell, Hell surely would have frozen over. I recall venturing into the tunnels under the yet-to-be-ren-

Woman trying to stay warm on the streets

ovated Union Station, hot coffee and sandwiches in hand, searching out persons who were homeless huddling there. Then we scoured around downtown looking for persons who were homeless huddled in doorways and on heating grates. Unlike many of these persons, I had proper winter clothing to protect me against the bitter cold. By night's end I knew that my informants had misled me. That was the start of our 41-year (1981-2022) collaboration."

Larry Rice interviewing Ralph Case, Pastor Ken Klingerman, and Jim

"I recall offering small and grand gestures in support of you and your work even after I left Missouri State Government in 1986. Small gestures included frequent visits, volunteering at your annual dinner, supporting your efforts with the press and public officials. Perhaps the grandest gesture was the establishment of a satellite clinic of Malcolm Bliss Mental Health Center at the NLEC. To my knowledge, this was the first ever example of a public mental health agency operating in a shelter for persons who are homeless."

"When I moved to Florida, and especially after taking over as President and CEO of Miami's Camillus House there, I so enjoyed your periodic trips to visit and view that work that we were doing. Trips back to St. Louis often brought us in close contact again, often facilitated by your son Chris."

"Let all who read this know that Rev. Larry Rice taught me everything I know about homelessness, but not everything he knows."

Jim Barnes, who was a Pastor and engineering broadcast specialist came to work with New Life Evangelistic Center to help build what became the Here's Help Network. This broadcast network ultimately consisted of multiple radio stations and television stations throughout a three-state area including Missouri, Illinois, and Arkansas. Jim Barnes said, "One of the most exciting things that I have experienced in my life has been the twenty years spent developing the Here's Help Radio and Television Network. This network is becoming a very powerful thing where a large portion of the mid-west is being reached for Christ. There is amazing history to each part of this network. With God's help we have acquired some and built others. To be able to reach out and help the hurting and homeless through the ministry of Larry Rice and New Life Evangelistic Center has truly been a blessing in my life and many others."

"There is a lot of power when God is working in our midst through the lives of people who may have started as an alcoholic or drug addict, some through a bad marriage, and others who were down on their luck. Many have grown and gone on to have careers from the training they received here. They continued to live their lives for Christ knowing that they have value and are important to God and to the communities they live in."

Homeless Mom with children

As 1984 came to close, it would have been so easy to have stayed away from the controversial issues of social injustice concerning the poor and homeless. Controversial issues often alienate donors, upset politicians, and create strife. Yet the New Life team knew that following Jesus into the suffering of the homeless as gentrification took over and destroyed the homes of the poor and elderly, they had to take action for the sake of the oppressor as well as the oppressed, we had to declare the Word of the Lord. As Proverbs 14:31 stated, "He who oppresses the poor reproaches his maker, but he who honors Him has mercy on the needy."

Living out the gospel of Jesus Christ through direct service to the homeless was becoming increasingly difficult. This was the result of local municipalities imposing codes that were hostile to the practice of the basic principals of hospitality.

We knew that when Jesus said, "When I was hungry did you feed me, naked did you clothe me, or a stranger did you welcome me" He didn't expect us to give Him the excuse that we couldn't do it because some city law forbid it.

Having mercy on the poor with proclamations of freedom and justice brought new challenges as time passed. Yet even in the middle of such struggles, all of us at New Life knew that we were promised to God and He would never leave us nor forsake us.

Larry Rice giving an elderly man a fan.

1985 was truly a historic year. That was the

13

year the New Life Evangelistic Center team, needed to raise a historic one million five hundred thousand dollars. This was needed to double the power of KNLC Channel 24 and build KNLC Channel 25 in Jefferson City.

Bill McConkey who created the development plan to achieve that goal recalls those early years at NLEC. "I first met Larry Rice when his office was a trailer in Wellston. He spoke at our church and Penny spoke to the Women's Association. One of our Sunday School Classes sent an offering to New Life Evangelistic Center monthly."

Jim Barnes, Judy Redlich, Charlie Hale & Ray Redlich in lobby at 1411 Locust.

"When the old YWCA was acquired — many friends of mine were on the board — Joyce Pillsbury, George Scotch and others. Joyce Pillsbury called and asked me to raise money to build Channel 24. A friend, Richard Collard led this campaign."

"In more recent years, I have been able to volunteer with the Development team and also the Fiscal team. God has used Larry through all these years. Larry has been obedient to His call. God has provided for NLEC."

As New Life moved into the month of July, not only did it continue to raise the funds needed for the television station's "Coming Alive in 85" campaign, but also for fans for the sick and elderly. On July 15, long lines of people over 55 years of age were formed at 1411 Locust headquarters. That day hundreds of fans were given away as well as 100 checks of $40 each payable to the electric company. These checks were to help those with shut off notices, keep their electricity on.

Advocates for the homeless marching to remind political leaders of the plight of the poor and homeless.

While the staff at the New Life Evangelistic Center was responding

14

to the emergency heat crisis by day, at night the homeless continued to come for shelter. The 2017 Park women's shelter not only had every bed full, but the floor was also packed with women sleeping on it. The pressures were building. We had to continually seek God, calling on him for help.

The NLEC Staff moved into 1986 with words from Philippians 4:13 burning in our hearts. It declared, "I can do all things through Christ who strengthens me." By the grace and power of God the New Life

Christmas at the St. Louis Convention Center bringing hope to over 4,000 poor and homeless people.

Evangelistic Center team in addition to caring for growing numbers of homeless people, assisting the poor and elderly during the severe hot and cold weather, continued working to double the power of KNLC channel 24, and build Channel 25 in Jefferson City.

Charlie Hale shares what KNLC meant to him as he grew up. "NLEC has brought me closer to the Lord. It has also taught me that God is always on time. New Life has made me realize how bad the homeless problems are around the world as well as in our metropolitan area. For the past 24 years, I was informed and excited to be a part of a new TV station coming to St. Louis. This was exciting because St. Louis only had 5 TV Stations to choose from and now Channel 24 would add a 6th. Plus, it was spreading the gospel of Jesus Christ."

It was in October of 1986 that NLEC had the first of a series of walks with the homeless from St. Louis to Jefferson City. In 1987 New Life began its work among those in need in India. Then as the year of 1988 concluded New Life Evangelistic Center hosted one of the largest Christmas parties in the St. Louis history. This party which was held

Line of people waiting to get into 1411 Locust Street in downtown St. Louis.

at the St. Louis Convention Center involved 1000 volunteers providing direct help and hope to over 4000 poor and homeless people.

It was experiencing this power of God at work daily, in the early years of New Life Evangelistic Center that gave us the strength, faith and determination to continue despite the obstacles that were encountered over and over. We witnessed time and again how God was faithful. It was because of His faithfulness, New Life Evangelistic Center was not only able to continue, but to be "more than conquerors through Christ who loved us" (Romans 8:37).

During the past 50 years God's faithfulness continued to flow through the NLEC partners who supported the NLEC teams who were serving Christ. The New Life staff daily shared with the poor and homeless the same compassion that had been provided for them through the resurrection of Jesus Christ.

Cynthia McCrae shared what it meant to her and her family to be partners with New Life Evangelistic Center. "My parents used to volunteer as a couple for years making sandwiches for the NLEC clients. I helped volunteer for serving dinners at the downtown building. I had never met homeless people before, and it was eye-opening to have seen so many homeless folks. I then started donating in-kind donations as much as I could."

Larry Rice praying for a man who is sleeping on a park bench – Street Patrol became another permanent service that New Life Evangelistic Center teams performed.

In 1989 the work of New Life Evangelistic Center was divided into four major categories. These were the services that were perma-

Christmas at 1411 Locust Street in St. Louis, Missouri

nent, those which were seasonal, other's which covered geographical areas, and special emergency responses to the needs of the poor and homeless.

The permanent services New Life Evangelistic Center had, involved the year-round emergency housing shelters, the farms for the homeless, the 24-hour hotlines which NLEC had in operation. These offered round-the-clock telephone counseling prayer and referral. In addition, there were the New Life free clothing stores, emergency food provisions, the worship services, and classes for those who were in NLEC's programs. New Life Evangelistic Center also provided the bi-monthly New Life ZOA Free Paper, and NLEC's Community Sharing Fund which gave assistance for the payment of utility bills. NLEC also had an eye clinic open on Tuesday afternoons.

The services provided by New Life Evangelistic Center on a seasonal basis involved the distribution of fans, screens, and air-conditioners to the elderly and needy in the summertime. In the wintertime, electric heaters, kerosene heaters, and wood furnaces, were provided, plus blankets, weatherization kits, gloves, and winter clothing. Those receiving the kerosene heaters and wood furnaces were required to attend safety seminars where they learned how to safely install and use these items. The weatherization kits included sheets of plastic, a roll of duct tape, pipe wrap and PVC foam tape. Winter patrols, where teams went out at night looking for the homeless in St. Louis and East St. Louis, also took place.

During the springtime, garden seeds and gardening seminars were provided so that the needy could raise their own food. Other seasonal services involved special celebrations for those frequently forgotten on the holidays.

Examples of holiday celebrations included New Life's special dinners and gifts on Easter, Thanksgiving, and Christmas for the homeless, fatherless, widowed, elderly and needy. On Mother's Day, along with meals the homeless were allowed to make free phone calls to their mothers.

Emergency responses by NLEC would vary, depending upon the criticalness of the situation. They involved helping a family with funeral expenses, emergency travel assistance, medical assistance, rent payments, etc. Usually these were not "Advertised" assistance programs, and each case was carefully evaluated. Some emergency responses take more time. For example, when the City of Times Beach encountered both a flood and dioxin crisis, causing extreme

New Bloomfield, MO

emotional turmoil among the residents, NLEC opened a center there and helped provide not only emergency assistance items, but also counseling and prayer.

The fourth area of service provided by New Life Evangelistic Center was that which were geographical. For example, in St. Louis City the center had an emergency housing shelter for homeless men at 1411 Locust St. It had emergency housing for women at 2107 Park Ave., and for married couples on Michigan Ave.

New Life Evangelistic Center also had two farms in Jefferson County. One was a 65-acre farm for homeless men, and the other was 135-acre retreat center for homeless women and children with the KNLC channel 24 tower and transmitter at this site.

In Jefferson City NLEC operated an outreach center for emergency shelter for women and children. Outside of Jefferson City, NLEC had a 40-acre tract that developed into a farm for the homeless. It was on that site where KNLJ Channel 25 was located.

We knew that scripture promised that, "He (or she) who is kind to the poor lends to the Lord, and He will reward Him for what He has done" (Proverbs 19:17).

In Columbia, Missouri, New Life Evangelistic Center provided emergency housing for women and children plus other emergency services at the Free store.

Solar Panels at the farm in New Bloomfield where Renewable Energy Fairs were held for the community. Participants learned about Solar Power, and many other kinds

Rather than starting multitudes of New Life Evangelistic Centers throughout a large area, NLEC worked through its television stations to establish care centers at local churches. These were not only more cost effective, but also involved volunteers helping those in need in their own communities.

In 1989, not only did New Life Evangelistic Center provide for the poor and homeless, but it also hosted a conference on February 17 to train others to do the same. Every Saturday evening, I would share a message with the NLEC Staff and the homeless at 1411 Locust in St. Louis. These were where the services were recorded and then broadcast on KNLC Channel 24, and KNLJ Channel 25. The printed messages were also placed in the ZOA Free Paper.

Many of the services that New Life Evangelistic Center provided those early years would continue. In addition, adaptations were made in the new world of technology that has taken place in the last twenty-three years.

Columbia, MO Freestore

An example of this is how the night out for the homeless that was held at one location September 22, 1989, was done as a virtual experience in October 2021. The Broadcast TV channels 24 and 25 became NLEC TV with NLEC now having social media sites like Facebook, Twitter, etc. plus its website at www.nlecstl.org. New Life Evangelistic Center also operates the Here's Help Radio Network, which is also on the NLEC TV App along with the streaming of the creation series and additional services.

As NLEC moved into the 1990's it worked to obey the Biblical mandates to follow Jesus Christ to the pain of the homeless and share His love in word and deed. This included direct assistance to the homeless and hurting, as New Life Evangelistic Center took the leadership to provide a social consciousness

that reminded believers of their Biblical responsibility to help those in need.

Chapter 2
Working for a Murder Free City

By August 26, 1991, one hundred and fifty-seven people had been murdered in the city of St. Louis. I knew then that we could no longer do nothing as more and more people continued to be murdered. After extensive prayer, I felt that if we were to follow Jesus into the pain and suffering these deaths were bringing upon St. Louis, a public call for prayer had to be given along with direct action to stop the murders.

Camping outside City Hall, Labor Day

New Life Evangelistic Center published a newspaper entitled "Working for a Murder Free St. Louis" where we issued a call for the public to join us in prayer. In the paper we printed the names of those who had been murdered. We asked for prayer for peace in the city of St. Louis where more Americans had died this year than died in Desert Storm."

Along with the call for prayer we also kept the issue of murder before the public. This included laying a wreath on the front steps of the mayor's house as a memorial service was held for the people killed in St. Louis. Pinned to the wreath were streamers bearing the names of the murder victims.

NLEC Started a gun swap program at the end of September 1991.

During the Labor Day weekend, myself, and some of the homeless camped outside City Hall as we planted crosses bearing the names of homicide victims. We also had a "murder-free fair" on September 6, to show residents ways to prevent murders through non-violent resolutions of problems.

As a result of the publicity being generated, more and more people started praying for a murder free St. Louis. It was later reported that from the evening of September 8, following the prayer of over 7,000 people until the morning of September 15, St. Louis experienced a murder free week.

New life Evangelistic Center also began a gun swap program where weapons were exchanged for assistance on utility bills. After New Life Evangelistic Center started its gun swap program at the end of September, the St. Louis Police Department began its Buy Back Program in the middle of October. It resulted in the buyback of over 6,000 guns. Police departments all over America soon started similar programs.

New Life Evangelistic Center and KNLC TV 24 then began training teachers and ministers to teach classes in non-violence. The curriculum for these classes included sessions entitled, "There's More to Lose Than to Gain from Fighting", "What Happens Before, During and After a Fight", and "Preventing Violence."

Matthew Carter with Mrs. Watts and Larry Rice outside City Hospital.

At New Life Evangelistic Center, we truly believed that no matter what the community problem might be, "With God all things were possible". As we prayed and continued to step out by faith, following Jesus into the suffering of the poor we continued to see miracles unfold daily.

Following Jesus also involved New Life Evangelistic Center requesting that the city of St. Louis allow the buildings and property of the old City Hospital to be used to help the homeless. Larry Rice and Matthew Carter along with others were arrested for "trespassing" on the City Hospital Property after mowing the grass in front of the hospital, their action was to publicly protest Mayor Schoemehl's awarding of the old city hospital to a developer rather than allowing the buildings to be used to help the homeless.

Pastor Matthew Carter shared his memories about his involvement at NLEC when he wrote, "I have so many wonderful memories about New Life – going to jail, sharing at the Saturday Morning Think Tank meetings, being asked to preach for New Life Evangelistic Center, the telethons, the Poor Have Suffered Enough shows, the voice overs for the scriptures, rides around the state with Larry, doing the video's at the prison's, the personal relationships with those whose lives were changed, doing tv during the holidays, the 140 mile walk, the tornado, and lots, lots more. But most of all, I remember the conversations with Larry about things, about God's work in us. And two stories that still loom big in my life with Larry is the fawn that we tried to save, and the woman who was a drinker we brought to 1411 Locust Street. She stayed for a week or so and went back to her old life. Those two stories seem to remind me that 'in the end' God is the only one who can fix things. In other words, we have loss, discouragement and disappointment in ministry, but we should never falter or quit because of it."

Reviewing the miracles and methods of the past can give us insight on how to address the problems we are facing in the present. This includes the present crisis of violence in St. Louis and cities throughout America as well as the issues of homelessness and other social problems. It was for that reason that New Life Evangelistic Center gave the State Historical Society of Missouri in 2019 it's past multitude of documents and publications when they requested such.

In October 2020 in an article in the Missouri Historical Review, A.J. Medlock described the Prison Ministry of New Life Evangelistic Center.

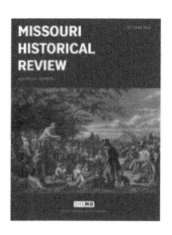

"In 1995, Reverend Larry Rice, founder and executive director of the New Life Evangelistic Center Records (S1236), housed at the State Historical Society of Missouri's St. Louis Research Center, document this period of NLEC's ministry and activism, primarily through Rice's correspondence. The collection also includes issues of the ZOA Free Paper, NLEC's outreach newspaper, and the Cry Justice Journal (later Cry Justice Now Newspaper), its publication for prisoners. Together, these materials offer insight to some of Missouri's most pressing criminal justice issues of the 1990s."

"Rice founded NLEC in 1972 to provide Christian hospitality to the homeless and needy through social service programs and ministry. Dissatisfied with what he perceived as the complacency of the modern church, Rice sought to put "faith in action" by serving the poor and homeless. As NLEC evolved, so, too, did its conception of Christian hospitality. By 1995, Rice had become increasingly drawn to inmates at Missouri's prisons, believing that they, much like the homeless, were outcasts of society deserving of Christ's love. To justify expanding his ministry to prisoners, Rice cited Matthew 25:36, in which Jesus says, "When I was in prison, you visited me."

'The collection's publication series chronicles Rice's early attempts to publicize the stories of the incarcerated. For example, the first issue of volume 26 of the ZOA Free Paper featured the story of Gayle Boone, a former paramedic in Montgomery County, Missouri, imprisoned at the Renz Correctional Center in Jefferson City for killing her stalker, Pat Hollensteiner, on April 12, 1991. In the article, "A Season of Stalking," Boone recounted the night Hollensteiner forcefully entered her home and attacked her with a knife:'

"I knew this time he was going to kill me. I ran down the hallway and went into the bedroom and grabbed the shot gun my father had given me. He was still coming at me, so I raised the gun to shoot. It misfired! Again, I pulled the trigger as he came close with threatening actions. The gun went off and struck Pat in the abdomen. He stumbled outside and fell in the driveway. I immediately called the sheriff's office and told them what had happened. Pat Hollensteiner was the Sheriff's nephew, consequently, and a few days later there was a warrant for my arrest for First Degree Murder."

"Boone claimed that the Montgomery County Sheriff's office had falsified and destroyed evidence, including stalking reports she had filed, leading her to accept a plea deal sentencing her to fifteen years rather than life without parole. Rice assiduously argued for Boones release by fasting, distributing pamphlets on her behalf, and urging the public to write on her behalf, to the Missouri governor Mel Carnahan requesting that he pardon Boone. The Missouri Board of Probation eventually granted Boone early parole in September 1997 after she served six years in prison. Although it is impossible to determine how much influence NLEC's efforts had on the board's decision, Boone expressed thanks to Rice and NLEC for their advocacy on her behalf."

"As word of Rice spread among prisoners and their families, NLEC began to receive a deluge of letters requesting assistance. These pleas resulted in NLEC launching the Cry Justice Journal in 1996. The newspaper contained essays, poems, and artwork by and about prisoners, giving them a chance to articulate their view on prison life and the criminal Justice System. One of the most prominent controversies covered in the paper was the Missouri Department of Corrections' decision in September 1996 to ship Missouri prisoners to jails administered by Capital Corrections Resources, Incorporated (CCRI) in an effort to stem prisoner overcrowding."

"Shortly after they arrived in Texas, Missouri prisoners sent letters to the Cry Justice Now Newspaper with stories of mistreatment by

CCRI guards. In one issue of the paper, Robert Goodson, a Missouri inmate at the Brazoria County Detention Center, Texas, recounted when CCRI guards released dogs on him and his fellow inmates:"

"I was right there getting kicked and stomped on, when that dog began chewing on Toby. I was only a foot away from the dog and I looked right into its eyes. And as this beast continued to chew on Toby, it looked right back at me — and it was a sight of fear that I would never forget. I was looking at hell in the face. And this beast knew what it was doing. And that was when I realized, as I was being stomped on, that this was no normal dog. It was as if that dog, that mauling beast was saying: 'You will be next'. I began to pray..."

"The Missouri Department of Corrections ignored NLEC's criticism until a videotape from the Brazoria County Detention Center surfaced in August 1997 that confirmed the conditions Goodson described. The tape, recorded by a Brazoria County sheriff's deputy on September 18, 1996, revealed CCRI guards and sheriff's deputies forcing inmates to crawl on the floor, with one deputy going so far as to shock one of the crawling prisoners with a taser. In another instance, a CCRI guard shoved a prisoner's face into a wall. The Department of Corrections responded to the outcry over the video by canceling its contracts with CCRI on August 22, 1997."

"Despite this victory, Reverend Mark Glenn, editor of the Cry Justice Now Newspaper, urged readers to forgive their persecutors as well as bless them, writing, "If we choose to hate those who hate us, then we are disobeying God . . . we must remember our sins made us enemies of God, until Jesus paid our debt, wiping the slate clean through His death, burial and resurrection." Humans could only overcome hate and evil, Glenn argued, by accepting Christ into their lives and "radically loving, forgiving, and blessing our enemies."

"Reverend Rice and NLEC believed that the call to love, forgive, and bless others extended to prisoners on death row. In volume 24, issue 1 of the ZOA Free Paper, Rice staked out his opposition to the death penalty, contending that by executing prisoners, the state of Missouri interfered with God's plan for their lives. More importantly, they executed countless nonbelievers before they had the chance to accept Jesus and commit their lives to Christ. Although Rice believed that murderers should remain in prison, he argued that they should be made to understand the sanctity of life, rather than be executed by the state."

Through the ministry of New Life Evangelistic Center, we daily shared they were all God's children. The homeless, the incarcerated, the poor, the fatherless, the widowed, and the hurting were all children of God. Each one of those who Jesus said in Matthew 25, "...that as often as you have done it to the least of these even so, you have done it unto me."

Yvonne Searcy shares, "I remember the NLEC Homesteading Program. This program offered families a chance to become homeowners. They were taught how to fix and maintain houses. Once the homes were up to code (city building codes). The family were offered an opportunity to purchase the interest free property making monthly payments to NLEC. After 6 years, the homes were awarded to these families."

As New Life Evangelistic Center continued to share the gospel of Christ in word and deed, God faithfully provided for the daily needs of NLEC. Janette Kruse shared a special miracle that had blessed her as she worked as Penny's assistant at KNLJ Channel 25. "Penny was a beautiful example of a Christian businesswoman. She learned to run the TV station and taught others what must be done to help it suc-

Penny Rice, Robert Reagan and Janette Kruse

ceed. She prepared Bible studies for the homeless men who were being served in their shelter. She hosted a television show to inform viewers of the needs of the less fortunate in the listening area. She was always asking for money to help them. She poured herself out to others. She was everything for everyone. She was wife, mother, the Boss, editor, teacher, talk show host, producer, and a friend to so many like me. She always amazed me by her tact. Sometimes her spontaneous ideas would just make me be in awe of her. She was such a true diplomat!"

"When I became her assistant and program manager at KNLJ, we became very close friends and prayer partners. We were a great team together."

"She taught me how to walk by faith. She trusted God to provide for her needs because, 'He had done it before, and He would do it again'. She knew that her God was not going to let her down. We would not have had that Christian Television station without her having fought to keep those airways on and shining bright."

"Things seemed to come up on a daily basis around KNLJ. There was never a dull moment. Phones were ringing, people were coming in and going out, the homeless men for whom Penny and Larry cared for had medical and dental needs. People were needing rent money, utility money, food money. There were those times when the Lord seemed to test our faith and try our patience, but it was at times like those that we learned to hang on to Jesus and trust Him at His Word."

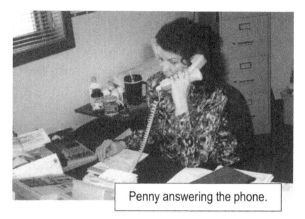
Penny answering the phone.

"Such was the week leading up to the miracle day. It's one that I will never forget. It had been so busy at the TV station. Calls were coming in and people were coming and going in and out of the office downstairs."

"I remember the morning that I climbed the stairs to our office and realized that Penny had closed the door. That was unusual. When I opened the door, I found Penny sitting at her desk with her head hung down and big old crocodile tears beginning to puddle in her eyes. She was troubled about something, but what??? I had seen that look on her face before, but this was a more serious look."

"She hadn't been herself for days prior to that morning, so I finally flooded her with questions as I SAID, "Honey, what is going on with you? I've never seen you act like this before. Did I do or say something wrong? Is something going on with the kids? What's wrong?"

"It was rare to find Penny questioning God and almost at a loss for words. She had to admit to me that morning that although she was trying to walk by faith, it was so hard. Sobbing, she said, "I just haven't heard back from God on this troubling situation yet."

"She didn't want to speak a negative confession, but basically, it was getting very close to the date she was going to have to do something about a very large electric bill that was due. That bill was around $7,000.00 and there were no funds to cover it. If she couldn't pay the bill, the television station might be shut down! She had about a week left as she said, "God has never let me down yet."

"It seemed the situation was so impossible that we decided to fast for the week. We had fasted together before. One of those times, we saw a man get a pardon from the governor. This was huge in Penny's eyes, and she never forgot that move of God on behalf of that man. So, remembering the outcomes of the previous fasts, we began to pray every day, many times a day."

"Penny would tear up at times and say, "I'm trusting you Lord. We're not going to be able to keep going and doing your work here if You don't come through for us this time again, Lord. You have done it before, and You will do it again, Lord.""

"At home, I used the 15 or 20 prayer cards and scripture notes that the Lord had been giving me for years. I decided to share them with Penny. They blessed her so much that she made copies of them, but since she could not read my writing, she looked up all the scriptures herself and learned them, too."

"As the week went on, we started to get the fight back in us and we started to get the strength and the faith of the Holy Spirit down deep in us again. We spoke His Word all through that week and encouraged each other in the Lord. It was so amazing! We only spoke words of faith. After some days, it was getting fun. I loved fasting together with her, praying and believing God to answer this 'impossible' prayer. We were getting over our nervousness and had moved into faith again. We cried out to God with tears of joy and expectancy at the same time. We needed a lot of money and we needed it "now". We knew that the Lord was able to do anything and to do it more abundantly!"

"As the day was approaching, it was getting exciting to see what God was going to do. $7,000.00 was a whole lot of money. We thought it might possibly come in a lot of smaller increments. Then "the day before" came and we were getting that butterfly feeling in the pit of our stomachs. We were excited and sitting on the edge of our seats, yet we were a little scared at the same time. I was crying out to God for my dear friend Penny and for a move of God. I was reminding Him that He was the only one that could do it, and that we were trusting in Him."

"Penny had thought that someone or a whole bunch of people

would have come into the station like before to give donations, but where were they??? There was nothing that came in the mail that day. We needed someone who would come in and possibly give the whole amount as a donation, but by now it was to the stage of the game in our thoughts that we were starting to doubt and to get a little nervous. There was nothing that had come in as yet."

"At the end of the day, we agreed to quote those scriptures and tell God about His promises throughout that night and into the next morning. I stayed up late praying and crying out to the Lord because I loved Penny, I loved working with her, and I loved my job which depended on being able to keep the station open by paying that bill."

"Then the next day came... the due day, the day of excitement and expectancy of our miracle for which we had been believing."

"It was my job to go pick up the mail that day. Penny and I just smiled and looked at each other with hope in our hearts as I left the building. I went down to the old post office and picked up the mail. There was always lots of mail and especially personal letters that came every day for Larry."

"By the time I got back from the post office, the office was hustling. The phone was ringing off the hook, and the other secretary was on the main phone, so I threw the mail on the counter and ran upstairs as fast as I could to get the call. After the call, I got busy at my desk notarizing and stamping the stack of legal papers I did monthly, completely forgetting about the mail that was just sitting there on the counter."

"All of a sudden, out of the clear blue sky, I hear THIS BLOOD CURDLING SCREAM COME OUT OF Penny. It scared me so much I screamed to her, as my heart was pounding out of my chest and I flew out of my chair to the top of the steps and yelled, 'Penny!!! What's wrong?!?!' She had just been going through the stack of mail."

"She was so out of breath by the time she got upstairs, because she ran so fast and hard screaming all the way, "You just won't believe it!!!" Thank You Dear Lord! I love you Jesus!!"

"We were so excited. All she could do was wave the check above her head and then hold it to her heart and say, "Thank you, Jesus! Thank you, Jesus!"

"Yes! It was a check for over $7,000.00. It was truly an on-time gift from a gracious donor who was definitely listening to our God... the God who was listening to our prayers, the God who wanted to bless our hearts, the God who wanted Penny to be able to pay the utility bill that day."

"It was truly one of the sweetest miracles that I was ever a part of experiencing because it meant that the television station would remain on the air, the ministry would continue to care for the homeless, and I would be able to keep my job. It was one of the most memorable times in my life. I will never forget it as long as I live."

As New Life Evangelistic Center entered 1998, it rejoiced over all that God had done in the lives of his children in 1997 as a result of those who partnered with NLEC. New Life Evangelistic Center at that time was a 26-year-old ministry, dedicated to Christian and charitable purposes.

NLEC continued through the love of Jesus, to reach out and help the poor, homeless, elderly, unemployed, incarcerated persons and their families and other dispossessed persons throughout the Midwest and through its mission outreaches in other states and countries.

In 2022, as New Life Evangelistic Center celebrates fifty years of following Jesus into the pain and suffering of the homeless. I thank God for every NLEC partner who faithfully shares with the work of New Life Evangelistic Center. It is these saints sent by God who have made it possible for the countless testimonies like that of Sonia's which was shared in the last half of 1998.

Sonia said, "I was pushed out of the car at 65 miles-per-hour onto the highway. My injuries were so severe, that I died on the operating table and lost my unborn child. I came back to life by the grace of God and awoke from a coma three weeks later. Even though I knew it was my Heavenly Father who saved my life, I disregarded this miracle and went right back to smoking crack cocaine with even more self-pity and denial. It was after my fifth arrest, when I got sick and tired of being sick and tired. I decided I would find rest by committing suicide. As I was walking towards the riverfront, I did not pay attention to where I was going, A car nearly ran me over. The woman driving the car blew her horn and was a mere two inches from me. When I looked up, I saw the KNLC Channel 24 sign. At that point, I remembered seeing Reverend Larry Rice on television, and I recalled how he helped the hundreds of Missouri inmates who were abused in Texas. I walked over to the NLEC office and was welcomed by Jake, a NLEC volunteer worker. I told him my story and my plan. He and several other staff members prayed for me and at that point I gave my life to my savior, Jesus Christ. Glory be to God!

In the year 2000 Victor Anderson wrote, "By seeking God's direction,

I found that God will do His part and can be trusted. He had a plan and a purpose for me and has one for you also; but you must seek his will for you and have faith in Him and believe in His son, Jesus Christ. He will fulfill your every need. "But my God shall supply all of your need according to his riches in glory by Christ Jesus" (Phil 4:19).

"When I thought all was lost, I was found, and now I see. Joining NLEC training program 10 years ago was one of the best things that has ever happened to me. I trained as a control board operator for KNLC TV 24 in St. Louis and KNLJ TV 25 in New Bloomfield, Missouri. I also learned about Electronics, TV-Programming, Editing and TV-Production which prepared me for what I'm doing today. Thank you, Lord, and thank you NLEC for this great opportunity."

Victor Anderson

Robert shared, "Over the years I have seen New Life again and again, step up and be an advocate for the homeless when others would just walk on by just like the story of the good Samaritan."

With God all things are possible. We would see that daily at New Life Evangelistic Center as we continued to follow Jesus into the pain of the hurting and homeless and show them through the power of the Holy Spirit that "there is hope for Christ is Risen".

Chapter 3
The World of Renewable Energy

2001 was the year when there were so many cries for help daily coming to New Life Evangelistic Center. Salehe Shaqboni pleaded, "My bills have been too much for my fixed income. The apartment is very cold, and I cannot take a bath, I must go to other places to eat because I have no way to cook. I also must pay for my high blood pressure medicine. I need help."

Growing numbers of people like Marcelene Cheers were crying out for help. "Because I am on a fixed income, I am unable to pay all of my bills. I owe $471 dollars and have called other agencies for help, but it always seems the funds are used up. We need all the help we can get. I can only get $17 dollars in food stamps."

Using Candles for Light

I can't afford to pay all these high utility bills. I owe $142 on my electric bill. I am retired and the only income I have is social security. It is really hard to pay utilities and buy food. I use candles and turn my gas down at night. It just doesn't seem to do any good.

Natividad Valdez

As I prayed what can be done to help all these individuals who were suffering as a result of their inability to pay their utility bills, I felt I needed to explore alternatives to the big utility companies. I also believed the NLEC staff needed to begin to teach the poor and elderly how to cut back their energy usage through energy conservation.

New Life Evangelistic Center was on the verge of a miracle. I knew that this miracle would involve more than just talking about the possibilities of renewable energy. It would involve directly learning about alternative sources of power and then taking the steps necessary to implement such. For that reason, I was so excited about learning of Solar Energy International. After contacting this renewable energy training center in Carbondale, Colorado I was determined to start attending their classes as soon as possible.

I took my first class in solar power in February of 2001 at the Farm in Murphysboro, Tennessee. As a minister I not only wanted to help people save money on their utility bills, but I wanted individuals to see that God wanted us to be Earth Keepers not Earth Breakers. This meant breaking free from the carbon fuels of oil and coal and developing the use of renewable energy like wind and solar.

The journey of New Life Evangelistic Center, along with my own personal life journey, would continue in the months to follow as I traveled deeper into the world of renewable energy. But that is only part of the story. In my own life God was trying to not only build a ministry of caring for His creation, but He was creating in me a desire to get to know Him better. This caused me to be awakened to God's second of Creation, His first book is the Bible. As I began to go on regular prayer walks in the cathedral of God's creation meditating on His word and works my faith began to grow.

The Holy Spirit moved me to encourage the NLEC staff to write a newspaper called Freedom Now. This newspaper by New Life Evangelistic Center was a publication that not only

DISCOVER ALTERNATIVE RENEWABLE ENERGY SOURCES TO SET YOU FREE FROM THE POLLUTING FOSSIL FUELS PROVIDED BY THE UTILITY COMPANIES

Participate in exhibits, discussions on renewable energy. Special events and entertainment for the whole family. Come be a part!

Sunday April 29

2 p.m. to 6 p.m.
Mid America Care Center
9810 State Rd. AE
One of the first of many Renewable Energy Fairs held at the Mid America Care Center in New Bloomfield, MO

helped individuals gain a new appreciation for God's creation, but introduced the community to renewable energy and why it is needed. As I traveled, whether it was to Texas, Oklahoma, Arkansas, Iowa, Illinois, Wisconsin, Colorado, Florida and Montana, I would bring a video camera and tape-record interviews with individuals and groups who were using renewable energy. These shows would then be aired on the NLEC Here's Help radio and television stations.

It was such a joy to see those who were previously homeless now in the NLEC training program not only learning radio and television broadcasting, but also how to install photovoltaic systems, mix biodiesel and utilize other forms of renewable energy. Their skills were featured at the renewable energy fairs NLEC held in New Bloomfield, Missouri.

From that small beginning in 2001 until the present the Holy Spirit has raised up www.missourienergy.org. As a result of this web site, NLEC broadcast stations and renewable energy fairs, thousands of individuals were not only introduced to the world of renewable energy but also the gospel of Jesus Christ.

In 2003, four years before Penny went to be with the Lord, the history book entitled Missouri: Crossroads of the Nation shared the following in its chronicles of leadership section:

Over thirty years ago, a 22-year-old preacher and his wife sensed God calling them to launch a ministry to the poor in the inner-city community of Wellston, Missouri. With only meager resources, Larry and Penny Rice rented a 50-foot trailer in a mobile home park and invited people into their tiny living room for Bible studies. They offered overnight shelter and food to the homeless, despite the uncertainty of when their own next meal might come. Yet miracles kept happening, and in January 1972, the New Life Evangelistic Center was born.

The couple's first outreach program was a 24-hour-a-day devotional telephone line called "Dial-A-Message." Seeing first-hand the overwhelming needs of the homeless, The Rice's decided to expand their operations. Several months later they were blessed with the opportunity to acquire a three-story former mansion built in 1869. And because the house was located in St. Louis, the Rice's were able to extend their outreach to the homeless, the elderly, the mentally ill and to prisoners.

"We saw a great need to reach out to people in the community. It has been exciting to see the growth of individuals and to see their ongoing legacies in the community," said Rice. "The ripples of our work now stretch far beyond our institutional walls. We want to continue to let the love of Jesus Christ shine through us to be a source of light and inspiration."

New Life Evangelistic Center continued to experience God's faithful protection and provision in 2004. As NLEC faced the need to raise $1,152,000 to complete the Federal Communications Commission requirements for KNLC Channel 24's to convert its analogue signal to digital, it also needed an additional million dollars to do the same with KNLJ TV 25.

This challenge to move from an analogue television signal to digital came at a time when the Holy Spirit increasingly led the New Life team to take steps to remove the "prosperity ministries" from its TV schedules. These were the ministries which promised individuals great wealth if they gave their money to these prosperity ministries. They promoted a message that wealth was a symbol of God's presence in one's life. This left the poor and homeless feeling they were second class citizens who God did not love as much as the wealthy.

Although removing these "health and wealth" ministries would cost

New Life Evangelistic Center $200,000 a year, action was taken to do such. NLEC believed that we had to follow the teachings of Jesus who consistently identified with the needs of the poor and homeless.

Esther was one of the hundreds of homeless people the New Life staff met every day who were in desperate need of help. She explained her need in this way, "I have five children and am homeless because of domestic violence. My family and I left an abused women's shelter in Pittsburgh, Kansas when my time ran out. Running from a very abusive situation, we ended up in St. Louis, Missouri with nowhere to go. I called the homeless hotline and was referred to the housing authority that helped me contact all the shelters in the city. No shelter we called had any space.

"We were totally homeless, sleeping in our van for two weeks out in the very cold weather. I felt abandoned by God and everybody else. I cried and prayed every night that we would find a place. My daughter was seven and a half months pregnant, and we were out in the cold van with a broken window sleeping under a few blankets."

A Mother and her children who found a safe haven at 1411 Locust in the Shelter for Women & Children.

"Then, Praise the Lord, someone told me about the New Life Evangelistic Center's women and children's shelter. I called the shelter and was told to be there by 4pm. I did that and that very night my five children and I were no longer homeless!"

"I will never stop praising God for how He delivered us off the streets and into a warm dry place. Because of the Lord, my faith, and the fact that I believe that "you can do nothing without the Lord Jesus," we are now warm at night. I have been at the NLEC shelter now for one month. I am working on my first goal, which is to find a place of my own. My children are back in school, and we have found a church to go to on Sundays' where we are able to have fellowship and teachings. I want my children to be taught in the ways of the Lord and to learn to praise Him!"

New Life Evangelistic Center applied to utilize the federal surplus property of the Abram building in St. Louis to help the homeless. Using this property at Fifteenth and Market in accordance with title V of the Steward B. McKinney Act would allow NLEC to help many more women and children.

When New Life Evangelistic Center applied to use the Abram building for the homeless, the city of St. Louis PR machine was feeding the media the line that a local developer needed the land the Abram Building occupied for a 1,500-space parking lot for the Kiel Opera House. The Mayor of the City of St. Louis, Francis Slay, was determined that despite Federal Law mandating this property to be used to help the homeless, he was going to see that it be used to create "City Hall West".

To achieve his objective of "stealing" the Abram Building from the homeless, Francis Slay fed every piece of negative propaganda about NLEC that he could to the Health and Human Services Agency that distributed the Federal Surplus Property. This included pointing out each time during the previous year that the police came to 1411 Locust. What the mayor didn't tell them was most of these visits by the police was to drop homeless people off at the shelter.

While the New Life Evangelistic Center did not receive the Abram Building in St. Louis, it would later acquire the former Social Security Building in Springfield, Missouri to help the homeless.

In December of 2004 God in His faithfulness met the needs of New Life Evangelistic Center after it no longer aired the "Prosperity Ministries". That month our Living Lord provided a mighty miracle when New Life Evangelistic Center received two $250,000 gifts from two special saints who remembered NLEC in their wills. It wasn't until August of 2021 that New Life Evangelistic Center experienced a similar miracle when $240,000 from an inheritance was left to NLEC. Just like in 2004 the Resurrected Christ provided a mighty miracle to meet the urgent needs of New Life Evangelistic Center.

The journey through life with all its twists and turns can one minute take us to the mountain tops and the next to the deepest valleys. I experienced such a deep valley when Penny was diagnosed with advanced breast cancer on April 20th, 2005. The cancer was very aggressive and had negative genetic and hormone receptors which meant it would not respond to Tamoxifen or Herceptin to prevent recurrence. However, the cancer in her breast did shrink 60% after 8 weekly treatments of Taxotere administered at Ellis Fischel Cancer Center in Columbia. Surgery at the University Hospital removed all the tumor from the breast with a lumpectomy, but active cancer remained in the lymph nodes under her left arm.

Soon after her diagnosis, Penny was in prayer as to how to respond to the devastating news that she had cancer. As she prayed, it became clear to Penny that she was not to focus exclusively on her own struggles. Instead, she was to reach out to other women who found themselves beaten down by the effects of breast cancer. Penny felt led to start a ministry to cancer victims as she meditated on Jesus' words, "Consider the lilies, how they grow..." (Matthew 6:28).

Penny's vision was to have several breast cancer survivors like herself become volunteer Lily Ladies, who would open a room in their homes to invite newly diagnosed women to come and be encouraged and supported. Those who came would be informed about how they could stand together in dignity and allow the loving hand of God cultivate a resilient beauty in them for all to see. Penny called her new organization, "Consider the Lilies".

Martagon Lilies which are trampled underfoot repeatedly, are very resilient and spring back

In September of 2005, the US General Service Administration invited NLEC to apply to use the former Social Security Building at 806 N Jefferson in Springfield, MO to help the homeless. NLEC applied for this Federal Surplus Property believing the opportunity was from the Lord. This invitation was in accordance with the Steward B McKinney Homeless Assistance Act that required that federal surplus property be used to help the homeless. This application was being made at a time of tremendous need at New Life. Despite these needs New Life Evangelistic Center applied for this facility knowing that God is faithful, and that He is in control.

THE VETERANS
COMING HOME CENTER
A DIVISION OF
New Life Evangelistic Center
"Working to be there when people are hurting"
(417) 866-3363

As NLEC moved into the year 2006, following the traditional New Year's telethon on KNLC TV-24, I had no idea Penny would be with me only fourteen more months before she went to be with the Lord. Daily I would thank Jesus for her and how He opened the door for us to travel together throughout much of 2006.

In January 2006, as we continued to shelter the homeless at the

NLEC free store in Springfield, we moved forward with our application for utilizing the former Social Security building in Springfield, MO for homeless services. As we applied for this Federal Surplus Property at 806 N Jefferson, we took every step possible to prevent our application from experiencing the controversy we underwent when we applied for the Abrams building in St. Louis. This meant not sharing the news we were applying with the local media.

Penny at New Year's telethon on KNLC TV-24

I thanked God February 6 for how He had provided $1,450,000 from the sale of WCBW and WDID radio stations to provide the money to move KNLJ TV-25 from analog to digital. We still had to believe Jesus for the provision of the resources to move KNLC TV-24 to digital TV but I knew He would also provide a miracle to do this.

In February, Penny and I traveled through Oregon into California recording TV shows on renewable energy. It was great traveling the Pacific coastline and then through the redwood forests. In Ancata, California we interviewed Larry Schlusser who invented the Sun Frost Refrigerator. We met him at his energy efficient home which was featured in Home Power Magazine. After visiting his home, we went to the factory where his Sun Frost Refrigerators were made and recorded a program there.

Penny was such a trooper. Despite her battle with cancer, she was right there by my side as we continued to do TV shows with those working in renewable energy throughout California, Arizona and New Mexico. In June we made a similar trip throughout the State of Tennessee filming those who were working in the field of renewable energy and sustainable living.

There was so much God was trying to teach me as I walked through the valley of the shadow of death with Penny. On October 20, I wrote in my journal, "Dear God, I am afraid to pray for patience lest more trials come. I know you desire for me to wait upon You! I am still wait-

38

ing for Penny's healing and a host of financial needs plus much more."

"The other day as I was walking around the pond outside the hospital in Springfield where Penny was getting her treatments, I noticed the contentment among the geese and ducks on that pond. I was wondering...if I was one of those waterfowl, would I have been running around worried about where I would find food for the next few days. I found myself crying out, 'Dear God, help me to have the faith and the peace that duck has. Oh Lord, you do provide daily. Help me as I learn to relax in Your Faithfulness.'"

It is one thing to talk about God's faithfulness, but it is something totally different to relax in His faithfulness. I knew in my head He was faithful but getting that knowledge into my very being or soul was something else. I wrote on October 24th, "Penny tells me tests show that there could be additional cancer developing in her stomach with more lymph nodes in her right shoulder. The news devastated me. As Penny went into the house in Marshfield I remained in the car and tuned into the NLEC radio station, KNLM 91.9 FM. Kesha's testimony was playing. Kesha was a woman who had been at Penny's Consider the Lilies meeting. She said, 'When the doctors give their diagnosis and it seems hopeless, don't believe that, believe God's Word. Trust the Word of the Lord. Have faith in God.' "Suddenly, like a bolt of lightning, her testimony struck me. I knew I had to trust in God concerning Penny and relax in His faithfulness."

As the Holy Spirit was working in me to relax in God's faithfulness, He was also doing a supernatural work in Penny's life. She shared that miracle on Tuesday, October 24th, when she wrote: "Tossing and turning, I asked God what was going on and why I couldn't sleep. He spoke to me, 'There is a rest in Me that is deeper than sleep'. Tonight, I am just crying out for His presence."

On Tuesday, December 19, 2006, Penny saw her prayer that the whole family would be together for Christmas answered. That day, Mom and Dad met us in Marshfield along with Jen and Nate, Stephanie, Justin and the children. Chris, Martha, and their children also joined us. Until the day Mom and Dad left for Texas, December 30th, we experienced one wonderful memory after another.

Penny wrote December 22nd, "All sixteen of us gathered around the table to eat Jen and Nate's homemade pizza. After that we gathered by the fireplace and Chris and Nate sang and played guitar. Then Jennifer gave us all her pictures on CD. She showed us how they looked on her laptop. They looked great! Then Jennifer and I watched

'Little Women' (a tradition). The rest either played dominoes or played Gameboy in the basement."

I was able to enjoy this family time as I relaxed in God's faithfulness. What a blessing it was for all of us to celebrate Christmas together. Little did we realize that this would be the last Christmas we would have with Dad and Penny.

On February 8, Penny wrote the final journal entry she would ever make in her life. She spoke of how she corrected my Bible study, donations she received, people she ministered to and movies we watched that night. The next day I had to rush Penny to the emergency room. She had fluid around her heart, lungs and stomach. A mass was detected around her liver and right kidney which the doctor was going to test to see if it was cancerous.

February 9 also was the day that Christian Television Network agreed to purchase KNLJ-TV 25. When the sale was finally concluded CTN agreed to acquire the TV Station for $3.5 million. This was a great answer to prayer. The purchase made it possible for NLEC to pay off the bank loan and have the resources to finish building digital Channel 24. Even as this miracle was taking place, I found it very difficult to see Penny's health deteriorating.

On February 13 it was obvious Penny was starting to fail quickly. I called Nate and Jennifer and they came the next day to be with us. That evening Penny started losing consciousness. I then put Penny in the car and rushed her to the emergency room of Cox South hospital. After examining her, the doctor informed me that the cancer had spread throughout her body. The day following Penny continued going in and out of consciousness.

On February 20 the hospital social worker gathered the family together and told us that Penny was hanging onto life just to be sure we were alright. She told us we needed to let her know we would make it. I went into the room following that discussion and told Penny once again how much I loved her and that I would really miss her but by God's grace we would make it. It was so hard to let her go. Nate and Jennifer took time to say goodbye as well. Chris and Martha sang "Far Side Banks of Jordan".

On Ash Wednesday, February 21, 2007, in Cox hospital I got up at 7 am after sleeping off and on in the chair next to Penny's bed. I went downstairs to an Ash Wednesday service in the chapel. Shortly after returning to Penny's bedside, I saw her take her last breath as she passed from this life into the next. I immediately ran and got the nurse who called the doctor. At 8:15 am Penny went to be with Jesus.

Penny had made a difference for Jesus in so many lifes like that of Mary Olle who wrote, "I've been blessed for years, moved to Richmond, MO and saw you had ministry in Springfield, and New Bloomfield, MO. I will always remember Penny for her smile and steadfast faith."

I hung on day to day after Penny's death by clinging to scriptures like Romans 8:28 where it says, "We know that in all things God works for the good of those who love Him, who have been called according to His purpose." All I could do was hang on and believe God was true to His word.

It was June 9, 2007, that my father's health was quickly deteriorating, and he was rushed to the emergency room. He had been in a rehab center following surgery when he had fallen and hit his head. At the same time, my father had been on a blood thinning medicine called Coumadin following his surgery. After the fall, bleeding had developed in his brain. When I arrived at his bedside my father was lying unconscious in that hospital room dying.

After praying for him and comforting my mother I went on a prayer walk. As the sun was setting and I was walking and crying out to God in prayer, He reminded me that it was a miracle that I was able to be with my father as he was dying. It had been the Holy Spirit who had told me before anyone else had known that dad was going to die, that I needed to travel to Texas and be with him at this time.

While I walked and talked to God, I also thanked Him for my Father's faith and that I could be with him at this time as he prepared to enter heaven. Two days later, on June 11, 2007, my father went into the eternal presence of the Almighty God.

My father did indeed love the Lord. Everywhere he went he would give out small silver crosses saying, "God loves You". I knew that I was blessed to have a wonderful Christian father and a loving wife who had trusted Jesus for their salvation. It was still so difficult to tell them goodbye, even though Psalm 116:15 says, "Precious in the sight of the Lord is the death of His saints."

I thanked God for the wonderful family He had given me. This included not only my immediate family, but my extended family both among the staff and supporters of New Life Evangelistic Center. Through the love and encouragement of these caring individuals, I saw how through it all, God is faithful. Words cannot express how much the encouragement of caring partners like Daniel, Michael,

Maureen, Larry, and Stanley mean to all of us who continue the work of New Life Evangelistic Center.

Daniel wrote, "I grew up in a church near my home. I heard countless sermons and Christian teachings, but still something seemed missing from Christianity as I knew it. Then I stumbled across Channel 24 and learned about New Life, Larry and Ray, and their ministry. What a breath of fresh air. This made sense to me! This is what Christianity should be about. Putting God's Word into practice. New Life has shown me what true Christianity should be. Thank God!"

Michael shared, "After researching NLEC I decided that they did the most for the homeless and those in need. Ever since then I have made donating to NLEC a priority. You are truly doing God's work! I have a bad leg and can't do much, but I donate to NLEC all I can."

Maureen and Larry testified that, "NLEC is truly a blessing. By the grace of God Rev. Larry Rice and NLEC has been a channel of the mercy and love of God to the homeless and poor people in our community. I think Larry Rice is a miracle worker and an example of the benefits of trusting in God. Channel 24 is good wholesome TV."

Stanley Anthony wrote, "I moved to Missouri in 1990 and to St. Louis in 2004, became familiar with NLEC's endeavors and participated in the outreach to locate and assist the homeless on the cold winter nights in St. Louis. We attended some functions, one in Collinsville and another gathering at 1411 Locust, where Slim and Zelma Mae were so faithful with their Gospel songs and Slims unforgettable piano playing. So wonderful to have NLEC throughout Missouri."

After the deaths of Penny and my father the challenges seemed to intensify. On the Sunday of July 8th, I received word from Jim Barnes that a person was on top of the 990 foot KNLC tower and rescuers could not figure out how to get him down, I cried out, "Dear God, please don't let him die! I have already experienced too much death this year with both Penny and Dad dying."

The previous evening, 19-year-old Matthew Gibson twisted his left ankle. He was in severe pain and asked one of his friends for a pain pill. Since his friend didn't have any, he took Matthew to a different friend's house who gave him something for his pain. Even later, when Matthew ended up in the hospital, they couldn't tell him what his friend had given him. All the doctors would say is that he had an allergic reaction to whatever he had taken.

Matthew took those pills around 11pm. Then he drove home in a company truck with his friends following. Not wanting to have an accident in that truck, he pulled in to the KNLC tower site. The next thing Matthew realized was that somehow in the dark with a sprained ankle he had climbed to the top of the tower. While up there he had fallen asleep on the top ledge. When he woke he was terrified. It was then that he started to earnestly pray, while trying to calm himself down and holding on for dear life.

After he had calmed down, Matthew decided to try to get down. He started down but almost fell so he climbed back up to where he was. He tried to yell down to his friend on the ground but couldn't get his attention. He climbed a ladder to the very top of the antennae, where there is a light. He used his shirt to change the color of the light hoping it would be noticed.

Finally, after 45 minutes he saw in the distance a light flashing back at him as if they were signaling him. After seeing that and hearing the emergency sirens, Matthew climbed back down to the platform below the antennae to wait for help. During that wait Matthew continued to cry out to God in prayer.

Five hours later with all the emergency vehicles present and failed attempts to communicate he tried to work his way down but the pain in his ankle prevented him from doing such. None of the rescue workers attempted to climb up to Matthew and there were too many guy wires for a helicopter to get close to him.

He saw a guy wire a few feet down from him and decided to try slowly climbing down it like you would a pole but at a 45-degree angle. So he started down with himself on top of the cable.

About 100 feet down he felt the cable starting to sway which caused him to flip underneath the wire. Matthew hung on there for about 10 minutes praying for help not to fall. He was terrified but yet confident that God was not going to let him die. By this point his hands were getting tired so he wrapped his arms elbows and legs around the cable.

Praying and fighting off the temptations of Satan telling him to let go, Matthew knew he needed to get down as quickly as possible. He then used his arms as a way to slide down and his feet to keep control and start sliding down the cable. At times he thought he was traveling at speeds up to 50 miles an hour.

Seeing the ground coming up fast he closed his eyes and prayed not to die. Suddenly he came to a stop only 8 feet from the ground where the rescue workers were able to help him.

Matthew was alive because of God's mercy and grace. As I visited with him in the hospital, with his mother at his bedside, we could not help but break into praise to God for his divine intervention. Truly Matthew was alive because God heard his cries for help and sent his angels to deliver him.

In August battles in St. Louis started developing on two different fronts in the work of New Life Evangelistic Center. One involved the neighbors in the 4700 block of Tennessee who were opposing NLEC operating a renewable energy center at 4728 Tennessee.

The other was beginning between the 13th and 15th block on Locust. The "call to arms" was spelled out in an article by Matthew Hathaway in the St. Louis Post Dispatch on August 26, 2007. Entitled "Down and Out in St. Louis-Homeless clash with Push to Gentrify City". The article was complete with a map showing the expensive lofts that were coming to the "loft district".

Hathaway's article stated that in "recent years, downtown residents and business owners have stepped up demands that something be done about the homeless, especially those in Lucas Park."

The mayor, following the release of the article, proceeded to close Lucas Park each day at 2pm for "cleaning". Later Lucas Park would be fenced in to keep out the homeless, allowing loft owners and their dogs to take over the park.

On October 18 following a hearing before the Board of Public Service New Life's conditional use permit to allow the alternative energy center at 4728 Tennessee to open was denied.

As the Fall days gave way to the cold of Winter, I wrote in my journal, "How I must find my satisfaction in the Lord. The longing and the loneliness seems almost overwhelming. How I need to relax in the presence of the Lord."

From the battles in St. Louis, I was now shifting my focus to opening the homeless veterans center in Springfield, MO. Linda Leicht explained this in her article November 13, 2007, in the Springfield News-Leader. Her article entitled, "Rice Seeks Quick Opening of Homeless Vets Center" stated, "The Rev. Larry Rice hopes to open a center for homeless veterans in a 'matter of weeks.'"

After battling the city of Springfield, Green County, and the school next to the center at 806 North Jefferson, what a joy it was to see this building open to help the homeless.

With the approach of Christmas, I thought about how Penny and Dad were with us the previous Christmas, but won't be here this year. I wrote the following, "For those who have lost a loved one, Christmas can be the loneliest time of the year. How I need Psalm 37:3-7 to un-fold in my life. Psalm 37:3 tells me to trust in the Lord and do good. Then verse 4 tells me to delight myself in the Lord and he will give me the desires of my heart. Help me Lord, to do this. Help me to commit my way to you for you have promised that as I trust You, You will make my righteousness be like the dawn and the justice of my cause like the noon day sun. (vs. 5) I can't see it now, but I know I must, 'Be still before the Lord and patiently wait for him.' (vs. 6)"

As I concluded 2007 waiting on top of the spiritual "tower" for God to rescue me, little did I know the challenge that would be taking place on January 19, 2008. It would be a slide down "God's guide wire" un-like any I had experienced before.

Chapter 4
In the Middle of the Painful Attacks and Storms Jesus is There

It was a bright sunny day on January 19, 2008. The Central Missouri New Life Evangelistic Center staff were decorating the assembly hall at the Mid America Care Center in New Bloomfield. Special decorations had been made. A catering company had been hired to serve the meal that evening as New Life celebrated its 36th anniversary. I was driving through a Jefferson County neighborhood knowing I would have to leave soon to arrive in New Bloomfield in time for that special event. It was around noon when I received the call that left me in a state of shock.

At the Mid-America Care Center in New Bloomfield a man named Matthew Watkins suddenly walked up behind Maurice while he was broadcasting music over the radio network. Matthew then pulled out a knife and proceeded to cut Maurice's throat. Matthew then walked out of the room and stabbed James in the stomach as he came through the door. Throwing down the knife, Matthew Watkins picked up a chain saw, and after starting it proceeded to attack Harvey. Then he turned on Bruce and cut his stomach wide open.

When I received that call telling me of the attack that took place I sped off to New Bloomfield. Even though I had put the pedal to the metal my thoughts were moving faster than I was speeding down Highway 70.

Matthew Watkins had been brought to NLEC by his mother and grandmother. When we asked his medical history, we were told he never experienced much more than a common cold. Later we learned that Matthew had been in and out of mental hospitals until his mother no longer knew what to do with him. It was then that they had brought him to New Life Evangelistic Center.

After receiving the 911 call, the Callaway County Sheriff's Department sped to the scene of the attack. An ambulance arrived at the scene before the Sheriff's deputies did. As the medics jumped out of the ambulance to treat the men who had been attacked, Matthew started to come at them with the chain saw. The medics retreated to the ambulance and locked the doors until the Sheriff's deputies arrived minutes later. In the meantime, Matthew Watkins went over to a black car that NLEC owned and with the chain saw cut into the hood the letters KKK.

Once the deputies arrived, they quickly took Matthew into custody and the medics proceeded to work on the injured. Harvey and James were treated on site while Bruce and Maurice were air lifted to University Hospital in Columbia. When I arrived on the scene, the complete parking lot along with the Care Center was roped off with yellow crime tape. This was the place where in a matter of hours New Life Evangelistic Center was scheduled to have its big anniversary fund raising dinner!

The 36th anniversary celebration was to have been the first major fund raiser New Life had had in Central Missouri since Penny had died. The dinner was catered, and Janice had even obtained matching uniforms for our men to wear as they served the tables. Now when our donors arrived, instead of being treated to a delicious meal and inspirational entertainment, they would be treated to a crime scene.

As I cried out to God for direction, I felt led to invite those who arrived for the anniversary celebration to the house across the street from the Care Center. This was the house Penny and I had lived in with the children years earlier.

Matthew Carter, our guest speaker for the evening, joined me in a special prayer gathering. We were all traumatized by the events that had taken place earlier in the day. Never before in the history of New Life Evangelistic Center's 36 years had we been attacked in this way.

The New Bloomfield staff and some of the donors (many had just returned home when they arrived at the crime scene) gathered in the living room and cried out to God. We prayed for Bruce and Maurice, that they would live, as we also prayed for Harvey and James. That living room became an Upper Room out of the Book of Acts where we sought God and His divine intervention.

As we cried out to God in the name of the Lord Jesus Christ, His Spirit moved in our midst. He assured us of His presence at this hour of trial and tribulation.

The days that followed were indeed a journey of faith. As we continued to pray for Maurice and Bruce who remained in the hospital, media all over the United States carried the story of the chain saw attack. When I was interviewed by CNN, I stressed how the Missouri's mental health cutbacks were resulting in mentally ill individuals like Matthew Watkins being left on the streets without treatment.

It was a day of rejoicing when Maurice was released from the hospital February 1. The medical report concerning Bruce was that the chainsaw cut across his stomach did not cut across any vital organs. One doctor commented that the cut was as clean and smooth as any surgeon would make.

Bruce, however remained in the hospital because of the infection that set in. For days he would linger between life and death as thousands prayed for him around the world. What a miracle it was when months later Bruce Calkins was finally released from the hospital.

During the month of October I found myself spending more and more time with Debra Lay. She was not only a person who helped me relax in the midst of stressful situations but she was also a woman who believed in the power of God.

Debra and I would spend many hours talking about the Word of God, daily events and our past. On one occasion as I was traveling from St. Louis to Marshfield, I spent the entire trip on the phone talking to Debra.

At the Veteran's Dinner that New Life Evangelistic Center hosted on November 11, Debra and I spent the entire evening interacting. People were starting to recognize us as a couple. After the dinner we visited some parks and talked and talked.

While I was spending more time interacting with Debra, I was also seeking God for new ways to help the homeless. In Springfield, Missouri this took the form of a special assistance program for veterans.

During the rest of November, not only did NLEC sponsor a large Thanksgiving dinner, but it also developed a Christmas Adoption program. This program featured on KNLC TV-24 involved needy families who would receive gifts for their children from members of the community who would adopt them.

New Life's shelter and training programs were growing as well as my feelings for Debra. When I asked her to marry me, she agreed. The date was set for February 28, 2009.

On December 19, 2008, HUD published in the Federal Register that the Federal Building Courthouse at 339 Broadway in Cape Girardeau was available to assist the homeless according to the Steward McKinley Assistance

Act. On January 26, 2009, Health and Human Services sent out instructions for applying for this building. On the same day, NLEC filed a formal written expression of interest in accordance with those instructions. All this took place while Debra and I were planning our wedding.

On February 28, 2009 Debra and I were married in the Chapel at Grace Church which had faithfully supported the work of New Life Evangelistic Center throughout the years. One of their pastors, Pastor Marty Haas, along with Jim Barnes and Ray Redlich officiated at the wedding.

The services provided at New Life Evangelistic Center in Springfield had increased during 2009. They now included additional classes, meals, laundry services, and an increased size of the free store.

On October 9 New Life Evangelistic Center had its annual Night Out with the Homeless. A rally was held followed by a telethon with Slim and Zella Mae Cox. Then teams went out on winter patrol looking for the homeless while others proceeded to bed down in Lucas Park across from the Library. Donations were raised

Slim and Zella Mae Cox

to help with winter repairs to 1411 Locust shelter while individuals from throughout the community got to know the homeless on a personal basis.

On January 12, 2010, the country of Haiti was devastated by a major earthquake which took the lives of over 200,000 men, women and

Mona Juste' in Haiti

children. For over 20 years NLEC had supported the Poor Children's

Assistance Project under the leadership of the Juste family in Haiti. After learning of this deadly earthquake I began to ask God how NLEC could be there in an even greater way among these hurting people. God answered my prayers and made it possible for me to go to Haiti in March of 2010.

When I got to Haiti, I discovered that three of the orphanages and eight of the schools had been destroyed that the Poor Children's Assistance Project had operated.

Upon returning from Haiti, New Life Evangelistic Center proceeded to increase its support in addition to sending a container with bunk beds and other supplies.

As New Life Evangelistic Center expanded its assistance in Haiti, I was thankful that God had made it possible in September of 2010 for NLEC to shelter over 130 homeless men, women, and children at its nine shelters in Missouri and Illinois. This did not include the 110 previously homeless individuals who were in the NLEC residential training programs. In addition to emergency shelters and training center New Life Evangelistic Center also had free stores in Missouri, Illinois, Kansas and Arkansas.

Because of God's goodness and grace NLEC was also able to provide emergency assistance for stranded travelers, individuals facing the shut off of their utilities, help people in need of food, funeral assistance and personal hygiene kits. As the winter months approached teams of volunteers went out each night to share food, blankets and Christian compassion with the unsheltered homeless persons living outside.

In February 2011 NLEC's Board of Trustees agreed to accept the donation of the former Overland Medical Center at 2428 Woodson Road.

The building was donated by OMC Building, Inc. and had been appraised at $1.5 million. OMC Building, Inc. was willing to donate the property to NLEC with the stipulation that we pay the current tax bills of $28, 526.26 and take possession "as is". Little did New

Life realize how critical this building would be in the future as the new administrative offices of NLEC.

In order to empower the homeless and help them in a variety of ways, my son Chris began working with the homeless advocates throughout the Bi-state area to develop the Metro St. Louis Coalition for the Homeless. This coalition was to be made up of not only the homeless activists and providers but the homeless themselves.

It was May 22, 2011, at 5:34pm, when an EFS rated tornado cut a path of a maximum width of one mile through the southern part of the city of Joplin, Missouri. Thirty-eight minutes later at 6:12pm the tornado with winds up to 200 miles per hour exited the eastern part of Joplin, leaving a path of death and destruction.

One hundred and sixty-one people died in the tornado with an additional 1,150 individuals injured. The tornado that tragic day in May caused $2.8 billion dollars in damage. This made it the costliest tornado in United States history.

Free Store in Joplin, Missouri

The New Life Evangelistic Center at 831 Moffit Avenue in Joplin was just north of the devastation. Five days after the tornado struck, I joined the NLEC staff in helping the hurting and homeless with food, water, clothing, and other assistance. As direct help was provided, I invited many of the tornado victims to share their stories on the Here's Help radio network and KNLC-TV 24. As these interviews took place, one person after another told me how God had been right there with them in the middle of the storm.

As I stood in the middle of the devastation that had once been the home of Thomas Days, he described for me what it had been like

51

when the tornado struck. Thomas said it sounded like a freight train as glass blew out of the windows striking his face. Even though Thomas tried to protect his face with his hands, he still experienced cuts across his face and hands. When Thomas looked outside and saw all the damage, he knew it was Jesus Christ who had spared his life.

As I talked to a nurse at St. John's hospital, which took a direct hit from the tornado, she told me how the walls started shaking as the tornado struck. She said it was nothing short of a miracle that she was still alive and walked away with only cuts and bruises.

Jesus was right there in the middle of the great Joplin tornado saving lives. It was a message I heard from one person after another as I interviewed these individuals who within a matter of minutes found themselves homeless.

Seventy-six-year-old Jerry Hodges was sitting on the toilet when his entire house blew away. As this happened, Jerry was thrown off his toilet which was bucking like a wild horse, into his yard. Jerry, with stiches and staples binding his lacerated body said he felt he was alive because he believed Jesus had something for him to do. Like Job he declared, "Before I had heard about God, but now my eyes have seen Him."

Myra Carr told me how she had hidden under her bed as the tornado ripped the mattress off the bed and flung it into a large tree. Although she didn't know why she was alive, Myra knew it was a miracle as she remained under the box springs that stayed in place. Myra had lived at that house which no longer existed for 30 years. She said that when the tornado hit, it sounded like an explosion. As Myra climbed out from under the bed into the devastation all around her, she knew Jesus had something special He wanted to do through her.

As the tornado hit Joplin with its deadly force, the NLEC buildings and staff were spared. When NLEC was started in Joplin in 1996, I never thought the city of Joplin would experience devastation like that. With the destruction of 2,000 homes, thousands were now homeless. Jennifer lost everything in the tornado and came to NLEC with her children. While she was there, she found clothing for herself and her children as well as other supplies which were provided through NLEC's free store.

After losing her home, Debbie was staying in her car until it broke down. She said she felt it was Jesus who had directed her to NLEC for food, shelter, and clothing.

Then there was Mary. When I first met this dear 83-year-old lady she was standing in the middle of a lot where her house once stood. Mary was in a state of shock as she asked me to climb a tree on the lot and get the one dress she still had which was caught in the branches. After climbing the tree and giving the battered dress to Mary, she clutched it tightly as she tried to hold back the tears.

I took Mary back to the New Life shelter. In the days that followed, the NLEC staff worked to help clean up her lot. The personal items that could be saved were brought back to the shelter and stored for her. I later learned that on the evening the tornado struck Mary was at church where she hid in the closet with 12 other members of the church. On Mary's 84th birthday, all of us got together to give her a birthday party. Mary stayed at New Life Evangelistic Center until permanent housing could be located for her.

I will never forget the summer of 2011. Not only had I seen and heard from the testimonies of those I had talked to of how God had been there in the middle of the storm, but I also saw His divine presence in the actions of His people. The legions of saints that descended on Joplin in the months that followed this tragic event clearly revealed that, neither tornadoes, nor "death nor life, neither angels nor demons, neither the present nor the future, nor any powers, neither height nor depth, nor anything else in all creation, will be able to separate us from the love of God that is in Christ Jesus our Lord" (Romans 8:38-39).

During the summer of 2011 not only were the New Life Evangelistic Center staff ministering to the homeless in Joplin, but also in other communities throughout Missouri, Illinois, and Arkansas. The NLEC free stores were receiving an average of 14,000 visits yearly from the poor and homeless. These individuals in need came in search of shoes, clothing, hygiene kits and other basic needs including small appliances, furniture, toys for the children, etc.

NLEC's 30-day, 60-day, and 2 Year Leadership Training Programs involved approximately 100 previously homeless men and women. They were involved in every aspect of the work of NLEC. This included the Here's Help radio and TV network, renewable energy programs, office and sheltering work, free stores, and much more with the assistance of over 50,000 shelter beds provided annually.

Encouraging the homeless to use their voices as a unified force took place not only through the acts of civil disobedience and press conferences, but through the NLEC media outlets. This included, in

2011, KNLC TV 24. KNLC was also carried on low powered community stations including Channel 17 in Marshfield, Channel 39 in Springfield, Channel 64 in Joplin, Missouri and Channel 54 in Green Forest, Arkansas.

Both by day and by night the voices of the homeless could be heard on not only the "Here's Help" TV programs, but also on the Here's Help radio network broadcasting throughout Missouri, Illinois, Arkansas, and Kansas.

In a society where efforts are constantly made to quiet the voices of the poor and homeless, it becomes increasingly urgent their voices are heard. The halls of power don't want to hear the cries of the homeless. Imperial economics is designed to keep people drugged so they do not notice the pains they are experiencing.

The policies of the rich and powerful are to block out the cries of those victims of the storms and attacks and see to it they do not get the shelter and other assistance they need. The religion of these power brokers is to see that no one will be able to discern its misery or hear the voice of God given direction on how to respond to the victims. I knew this was not the Biblical way. The solution involved prayer and giving the homeless a voice and then encouraging those who aren't homeless to listen to that voice and welcome them into their lives. As this happened not only would the homeless be empowered, but each one hearing them and responding to their needs would grow in their faith.

That had been the prayer not only since the founding of NLEC in 1972 but for each year thereafter. The Springfield homeless encampment in 2011 was just one more opportunity for the voices of the homeless to be heard by those who lived in the Bible Belt and claimed to be followers of Christ.

Chapter 5
Moving Forth by Faith on Behalf of the Homeless

If there was one word that I would use to summarize the City urban policies I had observed for the last fifty years in St. Louis, it would be gentrification. Millennials with money and most St. Louis politicians would define what I call gentrification as simply urban progress or urban revitalization.

Their efforts included the privatization of Lucas Park by the entity "Lucas Park Neighbors", a 501c3 organization whose president publicly announced that the NLEC 1411 Locust shelter would be closed by their efforts. After renovating the park, they began driving the homeless out each afternoon. The Lucas Park neighbors claimed it was to clean the park. Lucas Park is located immediately to the east of the 1411 building and to the north of the downtown library. As the homeless were pushed out of Lucas Park, the dogs were invited in, with the extreme northeast corner of the park declared "a dog park."

Most of the local media ignored the hurt and homelessness these "urban pioneers" were bringing upon the lives of the poor and elderly, who had lived for years in these neighborhoods. The gentrifiers only perpetuated the myth that as "urban pioneers" they were braving the dangerous inner city for the common good.

With the library investing seventy million dollars in improvements, and wealthy loft dwellers moving in, I knew that it wouldn't be long before these gentrifiers would start doing everything possible to remove the homeless and the NLEC shelter from their neighborhood.

Whenever a crime took place in Downtown West, or someone was observed urinating in public, the Facebook pages and email accounts of these urban colonists sprang to life, with every finger pointing at NLEC and the homeless. Homelessness became the new "N" word, as gentrification continued its racist policies in a politically acceptable manner.

The homeless who lived in encampments along the riverfront area came under increased pressure to move out. The encampments were called Hopeville, Dignity Harbor, and Sparta. These homeless individuals so desperately wanted a place of their own that they could call home even if it was a tent, or any other makeshift structure that they could crawl into.

I knew that the days of these encampments, which laid within the shadow of the planned Stan Musial Bridge, were numbered.

The criminalization of homelessness was well under way in downtown St. Louis. This criminalization made it clear no homeless individual could be in the parks after 10 p.m. It also did not allow outside porta potties to be set up for the homeless to use. When New Life Evangelistic Center tried to get a permit for a porta potty, it was refused. As a result, when a homeless individual had to use the bathroom outside, the neighbors who saw such would send out an email blast. The police would be called, and if caught, the offender would be fined $100 or placed in jail. If it was reported that a person was a repeat offender, on the third offense they could be sited as a sex offender for exposing themselves.

It was also a trespassing crime to go into a business to use the bathroom if the homeless individual had no money to make a purchase. Loitering in any area for an extended period in the Community Improvement District was considered a crime.

In 2012, the homeless could be cited for panhandling if they asked for food, money, or anything else. They were beginning to experience increased interactions with the police. This resulted in additional incarceration, and warrantless searches in and around Lucas Park and 1411 Locust.

As growing numbers of the homeless were coming to NLEC from surrounding municipalities, New Life would try to get additional shelters opened in the areas from which people came. It seemed though that the harder New Life worked to reduce the homeless population coming to NLEC, the more fervently the neighbors of 1411 Locust would complain about the shelter to city officials. As this happened, I knew it was my daily Bible reading and prayer that gave me the strength to continue.

On the first of March, Christine Byers, of the St Louis Post Dispatch, revealed that on September 21, 2011, Anna Brown had died just hours after she was arrested for trespassing. Anna was arrested as she sought medical help from St Mary's hospital in Richmond Heights, Missouri.

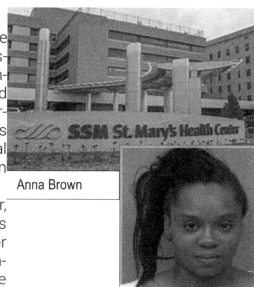

Anna Brown

Anna was a homeless mother, who had been to three hospitals in one week seeking help for her leg pain. On the night of September 21, she was in such pain she refused to leave St Mary's hospital, unless she received treatment. The Richmond Heights police were called. Anna was then forcibly removed form the hospital and put on the floor of a jail cell. Hours later she died. An autopsy showed that she had blood clots in her legs that had lodged in her lungs.

On Good Friday, April 6th at 10:30 am. I led a march from the St Louis County Government Building to St Mary's Hospital. Zaki Baruti and other community activists joined me in this march where we carried a large cross. At the conclusion of the march, a rally was held. At the rally two major questions were posed. The first was who was responsible for Anna Brown's death? And the second question raised was when would St Louis County government and St Louis County Churches take responsibility for their homeless?

As I was trying to get St Louis County and area churches to provide shelter for the homeless, I suddenly found myself in the middle of another battle on behalf of the homeless. This one involved the destruction of the homeless encampments along the riverfront.

On May 4, 2012, the city bulldozed the homeless encampment at Dignity Harbor. It was the first of three homeless encampments. The other two which were Hopeville and Sparta, were being destroyed by May 18.

While city officials took action to destroy the encampments, I began to see increased numbers of homeless individuals camping outside 1411 Locust St. I knew that another campsite had to be provided for them. When Middleton Carouthers came forward and offered New

Life Evangelistic Center two acres to use for such an encampment, I thought my prayers had been answered. On May 1 NLEC entered into a one-year lease agreement for $1 for the vacant tract of ground on the north side of Highway 44 at Vandeventer in St. Louis City.

At about 11:00 a.m. on May 16, 2012, members of New Life's staff and volunteers began erecting a 20' x 40' tent on the Vandeventer property. NLEC had one porta-potty delivered, on what had otherwise been a vacant property.

By noon that day, New Life Evangelistic Center began worship services under the tent on the Vandeventer property. By 6:30 p.m., City of

St. Louis Police Officers arrived to disperse all present and took me into custody along with NLEC Pastor James Potter, and two homeless men, Pedro, and Lee. The charges were nothing short of ridiculous. We were arrested for occupying a condemned structure. There were no buildings on the vacant lot, yet the city arrested us for occupying a condemned building. The property had been condemned without any hearing and while a worship service was taking place.

My wife Debra, Chris, Slim Cox, Matt Carter, and others who had gathered at the Vandeventer encampment site were present as the side street filled with police cars. After we were arrested, our hands were cuffed behind us with thick plastic bands. We were put in a "paddy wagon" and taken to a police processing station on Jefferson Avenue.

As the four of us were placed together in a large holding cell, James started singing praise songs to the Lord. Suddenly, we saw officers run by us into another room. Later, when one returned to check on us, we asked what happened. He replied, "A woman tried to hang herself with her bra."

Part of our booking had involved all our personal belongings being taken from us. These were then, along with all our money, placed in individual plastic bags. An inventory was made, and we had to sign a form stating the inventory in the bag was correct. After approximately two hours, we were transported over to the Justice Center across from City Hall on Tucker Street.

Once arriving there we were placed in a large holding cell with other inmates. As I shared the gospel, the jailers realized that these men, who were locked up, instead of feeling miserable, were starting to be blessed. I had a captive audience, and I wanted all the inmates to know Jesus loved them. I was then pulled out of that cell and placed in another one at the far end of the Justice Center.

By then, it seemed that news of my presence had spread through-out the jail. I was among my people, the poor and homeless. Each person I had met on the way to this cell was saying hello. Others quickly wanted to share with me some encounter they had had with New Life Evangelistic Center during the previous forty years.

When I arrived at my new cell, I saw that Pedro was there. I also quickly greeted my new friends who were locked up with me. It was great to be in "church" with these precious individuals of whom Jesus said in Matthew 25, "As often as you have done it to the least of these, you have done it unto me!"

I started praising God and talking freely about the resurrected Christ. The Holy Spirit was at work in a mighty way. Then, less than thirty minutes later, I was marched away and put in a small cell by myself. It was then I saw on one of the clocks on the wall that it was after 1:00 a.m.

When I was placed in my private accommodations, a wave of ex-haustion settled over me. I was so tired I didn't even notice how hard the mat was, or that the jacket I had worn in to use as a pillow was no longer available. I had given it away earlier to a young nineteen-year-old who was having a hard time being incarcerated.

As I laid down and closed my eyes, I felt wrapped in the loving arms of my heavenly Father. Then I quickly went to sleep. The next morning when I awoke, I noticed scriptures and prayers written on the wall all around me. I felt I was in a very holy place. Prisoners who had occupied this cell before me had scratched into the paint on the walls, "My God will never leave me nor forsake me" and "He is my refuge and strength" along with other passages and prayers. Some had signed their name and the date they were in there.

As I was meditating on these writings, I also found myself calling to mind passages like Romans 8:37-39 where it says, "In all these things we are more than conquerors through Him who loved us. For I am convinced that neither death nor life, neither angels nor demons, neither the present nor the future, nor any powers, neither height nor depth, nor anything else in all creation, will be able to separate us from the love of God that is in Christ Jesus our Lord."

As I rejoiced in the presence of God's Love in that jail cell, I was experiencing a new freedom I had never before encountered. Here I was locked up by city officials on a frivolous charge. Yet, the Holy Spirit was using this incarceration to empower me for greater service.

Jesus had turned something that Satan and his perpetrators of gentrification had intended for evil, into a mighty blessing from above. Later that day, all four of us were released.

Although sleep is necessary for survival, and is a basic human right, I was seeing more and more people losing this right as they ended up homeless. Individuals who were denied the right to have a place to sleep had a tenfold higher risk of developing depression. By the time many of the sleep deprived homeless arrived at New Life Evangelistic Center thoughts of suicide had increased.

I spoke to a homeless woman named Donna, who told me what sleep deprivation is like. "Every time I found a place to rest, I was asked to move somewhere else. At one-point police threatened to arrest me and drove me to the Justice Center. They didn't arrest me and give me a place to sleep; instead, they put me back out and made me walk a long distance back to where I had been. I got so tired my head was spinning, and I felt I was going in circles."

New Life Evangelistic Center's desire in the summer of 2012 was to serve Christ and His homeless and hurting children. It was Jesus who had enabled NLEC to continue to welcome anyone who found themselves in need of shelter, while other agencies controlled by government funding turned them away. This trust in God's ability to provide for New Life's daily needs kept it from being controlled by the political powers. Once New Life Evangelistic Center had spoken out against the injustices in the local community, these government powers would have cut off the funding. Because NLEC trusted God to provide, it was free to do God's work and will according to the mandates of scripture.

When a person doesn't have a place where they can be rooted and grounded in love and security, they will feel like tumble weeds blowing aimlessly across the desert of life. Becca said if New Life Evangelistic Center had not been able to provide her and her family with a place after they became homeless, she with her mother and children would have been forced to sleep in their van and car. Becca went on to say, "This would have led to my kids being taken by the Division of Family Services. Our van and car would have been impounded, and my mom and I would have been thrown in jail. I don't' want to lose my children and my mom."

People who were previously without a place were asked, after being homeless, "what does it mean to you to be in the NLEC Family and have a place to call home at 1411 Locust?" Amy said, "It means a lot to me because otherwise I might have to sleep outside, and that is not safe for a woman or a man. I would probably be drinking in the park and getting into trouble." Bill said, "It's good to be a part of a Christian Community and helping the homeless."

Unless a person has been uprooted, they really wouldn't understand what it meant to individuals like Carol to have a place to call home at New Life Evangelistic Center. She wrote, "It feels great to finally have a place where I feel wanted and loved and needed to do God's work." Debra said, "It's a blessing to have a safe place to go where there is no crime."

These individuals, who were once homeless, had found a place at New Life with brothers and sisters who were letting the love of Christ flow through them. Dwight wrote, "At NLEC I have found a place to fellowship, worship, work and build a more positive perspective." Victoria said, "When I didn't have anywhere else to go, New Life opened its doors for me and welcomed me."

As we moved through the Summer of 2012, I noticed more and more homeless people camping on the sidewalks of Locust, between 14th and 15th street. I was surprised the police and city officials would allow this activity to take place. Then, on Wednesday, September 5, it became clear that what I was observing was a plan by St. Louis power-er brokers to create a cause to shut down the New Life Evangelistic Center shelter for the homeless at 1411 Locust.

It was September 5 when city officials announced the cleanup of the problem they had allowed to occur. Now the gentrifiers could turn the public against New Life Evangelistic Center and call for the shutdown of 1411 Locust.

During the past few years, I had witnessed local governments place increasing restrictions on churches, faith-based organizations, and others who wanted to provide the homeless men, women, and children with shelter. In Springfield, MO I had seen legislation passed that required shelters to be located three quarters of a mile away from each other. Cities like Belleville, IL put such unreasonable requirements on overnight shelters that the Salvation Army closed its shelter in that community.

Municipalities throughout St. Louis and St. Charles County along with other cities throughout the Bi-state area, had all but outlawed shelters. Local police departments proceeded to threaten the homeless people that they found with arrest. Those who weren't threatened were often taken to New Life Evangelistic Center at 1411 Locust in St. Louis.

On September 6, the city of St. Louis Streets Department, under orders from the Mayor's Office proceeded to barricade all the sidewalks between 14th and 15th street on Locust. The signs placed on these barricades said, "Sidewalk closed for Health and Safety Reasons".

As the battle intensified against the homeless, New Life Evangelistic Center lost two of its courageous warriors. The first was Slim Cox, who died on September 11. Slim and his wife Zella Mae were champions of the homeless. They would come regularly and sing on KNLC for telethons to help raise money to help the homeless. The Coxes, who had recorded over 200 songs, were not only great supporters of the New Life Evangelistic Center, but also dear friends of the Rice family.

Lary & Cindi Walburn

The second warrior, who was consistently on the front lines for Jesus in the work of NLEC, was Cindi Walburn. Cindi and her husband, Lary Walburn, directed New Life Evangelistic Center's work in Potosi, Missouri. While Lary was working with the men in the NLEC training program, he also managed the NLEC Potosi radio station. Cindi was in charge of the free store where she shared the love of Jesus with everyone who came in for clothing. Cindi also organized special events like the big NLEC Washington County Christmas Party. The homeless in Washington County could always depend on Cindi in their time of need.

When Cindi died, October 30, heaven gained an angel while earth lost a saint. It was Cindi who I would frequently call when I personally needed special prayer. She was a great prayer warrior.

As these special saints went to be with the Lord, homeless individuals like Louis Broadway would continue to look for some sleep. The only place Louis could find sleep on July 27 was in a St. Louis alley. That night, someone poured gas on him and set him on fire as he slept. By January of 2013, 39-year-old Louis was still in the hospital. As he drifted in and out of consciousness the gentrifiers and St. Louis officials continued plotting to shut down the last major walk-in shelter in Mid-America.

The enemies of the homeless were planning ways to create in the public mind a negative image of both the homeless and the Christ centered work of the New Life Evangelistic Center. The planned chaos of phase one was completed. They had succeeded in first letting the homeless sleep on the sidewalks during the summer of 2012. Then, as trash piled up, they had worked with the police and the street department to remove the homeless and barricaded the sidewalks.

Now the condo owners and the developers, who were plotting the shutdown of 1411 Locust, were getting ready for round two in their efforts to get the homeless out of sight and out of mind.

As the pressures increased to shut down 1411 Locust, the need for shelter for the homeless increased. In May 2013, the Salvation Army closed its Harbor Light homeless shelter at 3010 Washington. At that location, Harbor Light provided 62 beds for homeless men.

As I continued to pray for solutions to the ever-growing numbers of people who were coming to NLEC at 1411 Locust, I felt the time had come to once again lead a march from that facility to the state capitol in Jefferson City, MO. The plan was to stop at churches in route, hold rallies, and hopefully get churches along the way to start homeless shelters in their communities.

Chris Aaron Rice, my grandson, and the youngest walker to complete the total walk reflected on the impact this walk had in his life: "The cause I demonstrated for was a good one. I was raising awareness for the homeless crisis in St. Louis. For nine days I walked across the countryside learning that there is nothing like a long walk for quality conversations. The people and their stories became real, tangent, and personal. I found I could focus on others and what they said."

"The second thing I learned was we have ingrained perceptions of others even before we meet them. I knew I would be walking with homeless people. Before I even began, I had a set image of what this would look like. Throughout the walk, time and time again, that image was destroyed. I realized my preconceived ideas can and should be changed. It was all about slowing down that caused this shift."

Chris Aaron Rice and Matthew Carter

"Finally, I learned that there is no better place to draw closer to God than on a walk. He meets us on every step of the way. My thoughts were sharper and more clearly expounded on that walk. I learned about who God was to each of the participants. I grew closer to Him through the lives of others. The walk from St. Louis to Jefferson changed me."

Reverend J. Matthew Carter, who was instrumental in the planning and execution of NLEC's Walk to Make a Difference, wrote: "The walk to Jefferson City made a difference in my life. I can also say that about some of the other walkers who were with me. I know one of them has gone into work for missions in several countries and has married a missionary from South Africa. Still others have gone on to do 'Greater Works for God!' I know that God blessed all of those who supported and participated in the walk."

"There are so many special memories about the walk, but most importantly, the special thanks and prayers each day that I continue to share for the churches. They made each day's walk possible by feeding us each evening, supporting us through prayer, letting us refresh ourselves and sleep in their buildings at night. These include the pastors and members of Gateway Central Church of the Nazarene, Bridgeton, MO: First United Methodist Church, St. Charles, MO; Court Street United Methodist Church, Fulton, MO; the men at New Life, New Bloomfield; and Wesley Memorial United Methodist Church in Jefferson City, MO."

It was on August 27th that we finally saw a victory in one of our legal battles against the city of St. Louis. On that day, the United States Judge Henry Edward Autrey ordered the city of St. Louis, and its officers and agents to no longer implement the emergency condemnation order of the property at Hwy. 44 and Vandeventer.

What an encouragement this order was to all of us at the New Life Evangelistic Center. That day of August 27 I concluded my journal by declaring, "What a victory, Jesus is Lord. How I thank Him for His faithfulness. By the goodness and grace of God we were also able to meet the pressing financial needs. What a mighty God we serve."

The gentrifiers had gotten a majority of the loft dwellers at 15th and Locust to sign petitions to have NLEC's permit to shelter the homeless at 1411 Locust removed. Hearings before the Board of Public Service were to begin.

At the hearing before the Board of Public Service on November 11th I testified that all the way back to Abraham when he welcomed three strangers, through the whole Exodus period, Deuteronomy, and the rest of the scriptures, the provision of shelter is stressed. I pointed out that at New Life Evangelistic Center we followed the scriptures and the teachings of Jesus Christ, not Mayor Francis Slay or anybody else. If that creates a clash, then we will have to continue to go through the courts saying we don't need a hotel permit. We are not a hotel; we are a church.

As the hearings before the Board of Public Service continued to progress, throughout 2013 and into the New Year the crisis among the homeless continued to grow. Even according to the city's own statistics through the end of November, 14,155 people requested shelter at the city and county funded shelters. Of those, 73%, including 4,691 children, were unable to be referred to any place. This had grown from the 51% of the homeless who were denied shelter due to overcrowding in earlier years.

The fact was that even as more of the homeless were not receiving shelter at this time, St. Louis City officials, bowing before the idols of gentrification, continued to move ahead with their efforts to shut down New Life Evangelistic Center's work at 1411 Locust in St.Louis.

Chapter 6
Following Jesus into the Midst of Adversity

It was a bitter cold day on January 5, 2014. As snow was falling, Benjamin was discharged from St. Louis University Hospital. With no place to call home, he walked from the hospital on Grand Avenue to New Life Evangelistic Center at 1411 Locust Street. This was the facility that St. Louis City officials in cooperation with downtown developers and loft owners at 15th and Locust were determined to shut down.

When Ben finally arrived at the 1411 Locust building, his feet were soaking wet from the snow and were starting to freeze. His shoes were cracked and falling apart. At NLEC Ben not only received a place to sleep, but food and a pair of new winter boots.

Darlene

Ben was not alone when it came to urgently needing the services of New Life Evangelistic Center. There was also Darlene, who ended up homeless when she could not pay the rent. She was turned away from other shelters because she was legally blind and had difficulty going up and down stairs. Darlene was told repeatedly by these shelters that they could not help her because she was disabled! Darlene was strongly convinced that she would have died if she had not been able to get into the 1411 Locust facility.

A mother with her two children.

The ones who wanted the 1411 Locust building closed, because they didn't want "those homeless people" in the neighborhood, could have cared less what happened to Ben, Darlene, Vernell and hundreds like them, who depended on New Life Evangelistic Center for survival.

Vernell, after losing her apartment, ended up sleeping outside a church in St. Louis with her two children. The temperature kept dropping during the cold January nights as Vernell and the children tried to survive in the frigid temperatures. As Vernell desperately searched for a place to go that would help her get out of the cold, she was told about New Life Evangelistic Center at 1411 Locust in St. Louis. Once she arrived there, Vernell and her children found warmth and love.

February 12, 2014, I wrote the following to the New Life Evangelistic Center partners. "Because of your generous support in 2013, 80,750 shelter beds were provided for over 5,870 men, women, and children at just the 1411 Locust outreach center in St. Louis. In addition, a wide range of on-the-job training programs were provided to help the homeless and hurting to be set free from the cycle of homelessness."

"With the severe cold weather, and government cutbacks more and

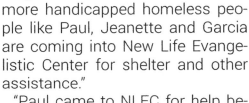

Paul

more handicapped homeless people like Paul, Jeanette and Garcia are coming into New Life Evangelistic Center for shelter and other assistance."

"Paul came to NLEC for help because someone ran over him with their car and broke his leg. He later dragged himself to the doors of New Life Evangelistic Center after he was released from the hospital. While Paul was at New Life, he received a desperately needed wheelchair as well as clothes, food and a warm place to stay. Paul said, "I am so thankful for New Life Evangelistic Center. The people there saved my life. Without their help, I would not have survived."

Jeanette came to NLEC after she had suffered a stroke and the hospital sent her to New Life where she awoke five days later. While she was at the shelter, she discovered she had a new family at NLEC who cared about her. Jeanette became part of the New Life Leadership

Jeanette

a

Training Program. She says, "Because of New Life Evangelistic Center, I know that God loves me and cares about me. I now have the opportunity to help others every day."

With God's love at work through the provision of a home at NLEC, Brian wrote, "To stay here makes the transition back into society that much easier. It is great knowing you have a place like New Life that you can go to after a hard day of work. The support you get being rooted in one place helps ease the burden of not knowing where your next meal is coming from or where you are going to sleep. God's love is working through His people at NLEC, and it all comes together when you are rooted in one place."

On the evening of Friday, October 3, New Life Evangelistic Center held an open house, a rally and a reception at 1411 Locust in St. Louis. The event consisted of visitors from throughout the greater St. Louis area who came to the 1411 Locust facility. This great evening of interaction and inspiration started at 6:00 pm and concluded with a midnight prayer gathering. It helped mobilize individuals and churches from throughout the Bi-State area to pray and organize for the upcoming Board of Public Service meeting.

As tensions among politicians and developers continued to increase, so did the financial needs. Sunday, November 2, 2014, I cried out to God in prayer, "I'm continuing to look to you for help. The Spiritual labor pains are so intense. The needs are so great. For over two and a half weeks now we have not had the money to pay the employees as well as many other bills.

"In the precious name of Jesus, please let the money flow in now, in order that we may be able to pay the employees, the other bills NLEC owes, as well as pay off loans. Jesus, we need your divine intervention now. There are so many people who need help with their utility bills, bus tickets, and other emergency needs. I believe Lord you are birthing something new at NLEC. Please let it come forth now."

The next day God miraculously continued to reveal His faithfulness as He provided a widow who dropped off a check at New Life Evangelistic Center for $19,700. Smaller donations also came in that Monday. Nine thousand dollars more came in on Tuesday and Wednesday. Then on Thursday, November 6, the heavens continued to open as $18,000 came in through the mail, with an additional $15,000 from one couple. What an answer to prayer. We were able to pay NLEC Staff, along with many bills, as New Life continued to help many who were facing crisis situations.

Two days before Christmas, the Board of Public Service voted that New Life Evangelistic Center would have to reduce its number to 32 individuals.

Immediately upon hearing the verdict, those in attendance started shouting, "Homeless Lives Matter!"

I was quoted on St. Louis Public Radio saying, "As long as they continue to operate that all-white board, you're going to see anyone who's African-American or [who] is helping African-Americans who don't have money, shoved out of the community. They tell me we have until May 12. God has told me I'm supposed to shelter the homeless. I have to choose between obeying God and man."

I made it clear after the meeting that New Life Evangelistic Center would be appealing this ruling to state and federal courts.

On Christmas Eve, December 24, I spent six hours outside the St. Louis City Hall with homeless advocates protesting the Board of Public Service decision. Then the next day, Christmas Day, I joined the NLEC Staff and volunteers in feeding over five hundred and seventy homeless and hurting people at 1411 Locust. It was so encouraging to join hundreds of volunteers in celebrating the birth of Christ by helping those in need.

While the city of St. Louis' Board of Public Service, under the direction of Mayor Francis Slay, gave NLEC the gift of ordering 90% of its clients to be locked out of the shelter, I knew that we had to help the homeless at all costs. We were marching to a different drum beat than that ordered by City Hall. It was the drum beat of the Christ of Christmas who said, "As often as you have done it to the least of these you have done it unto me." With that in mind, we continued to follow Christ into the pain and suffering of the homeless as we moved into the New Year.

In 2015 pushing the poor, elderly and homeless out of the neighborhood was called economic development. In actuality it was gentrification, which involved the robbing of the poor and giving their property to the gentry (or the rich). The result of this gentrification in January 2015 was clearly seen on Locust Street between 13th and 15th Street. Homeless individuals once gathered in Lucas Park, which was located in that area with their children. Now millennials with money have pushed them out of the park so they could run their dogs in that park.

The gentrifiers didn't stop there. They did everything they could to shut down the New Life Evangelistic Center Church. Their methods included attributing crime in the immediate neighborhood to the homeless. These haters of the homeless consistently fed the media and local politician's rumors that the 1411 building was a nuisance property. At the same time, these gentrifiers tried to destroy New Life Evangelistic Center financially with legal burdens and using social media to tell the community not to donate to NLEC.

The daily struggles and victories were reflected in the following journal entry I made on September 5, 2015. "I praise God for how He faithfully provided the financial resources needed this week. Then on Thursday, September 3, the attorneys met Federal Judge Ross and he said he was going to extend the trial date for a month and encourage all the parties to negotiate."

Little did I know the behind-the-scenes manipulation that the Slay Administration was engaging in. This took the form of letting New Life Evangelistic Center believe that if it made formal applications for permits, it could continue to have church services, keep the KNLC TV studios open, and provide a wide range of other services for the homeless during the day, as NLEC continued to pursue providing overnight shelter through the courts.

On July 29th Ray Redlich proceeded to submit the necessary applications for permits for NLEC to operate a free store, television studios, worship service and day center services for the homeless. This was done even though there was still no agreement with the city as the NLEC Leadership had met on several occasions with the St. Louis City's operational manager, Todd Waltermann.

New Life Evangelistic Center continued to work to get the necessary permits to reopen 1411 Locust building. On October 26 Ray Redlich wrote the St. Louis Building Commissioner Frank Oswald, "Thank you for your October 12, 2015, letter concerning the exemptions we requested. We would like to know as soon as possible if the City will grant us the exemptions at issue, since we are currently spending substantial sums to meet the City's other requests relating to our permit application. We are in a difficult position. In order to obtain the permit, the City has asked us to spend significant funds to make our building comply with certain codes without telling us if the City will actually grant an exemption to receive a homeless shelter permit."

"Also, along with the two City Code requirements mentioned in your letter (plat and petition; 500-foot spacing from schools), we are also requesting an exemption from the City Code's apparent prohibition against a homeless shelter being within 500-feet of a church. Since

New Life is a church, it appears that is another prohibition in which we will need a waiver."

On October 27th Judge John A. Ross issued his memorandum and order. In summary it stated, "Specifically, the record reflects that New Life applied for a new permit on July 29, 2015, during this litigation, and that the new application is currently pending before the city. There is not any indication on the record that the application has been fully processed or that New Life has received a denial."

"The Court has determined that the underlying RLUIPA and section 1983 claims are not ripe for adjudication and, while a declaratory judgement claim may stand alone, the Court is unable to determine the relative rights of the Parties while the application is still pending. Accordingly, the Court finds that until a final decision is made on the application, there is not a substantial controversy between the Parties to warrant the issuance of a declaratory judgement and will dismiss Count VII without prejudice", and the declaratory judgement claim (Count VII) are not ripe for adjudication and the Court declines to exercise jurisdiction over the state law claims (Counts IV-VI), this action is DISMISSED without prejudice."

After Judge Ross gave his Memorandum and Order, Todd Waltermann from the Mayor's office suddenly stopped meeting with us. Building Commissioner Frank Oswald then used the NLEC permit application process as an excuse to send inspector after inspector into the 1411 Locust building.

As the battles by the gentrifiers and the politicians continued to intensify, I found strength daily through the reading of the scriptures, prayer and the support of the New Life Evangelistic Center Community.

On Thanksgiving Day, November 26, 2015, hundreds of volunteers

Thanksgiving Day, 2015

from all walks of life served over 500 homeless and hurting people a delicious Thanksgiving dinner. Following this great event of feast and fellowship, the Jesus statue, which had been installed just a few days earlier in front of 1411 Locust was dedicated. At this dedication, which Federal Judge Richard Webber was present at, the Holy Spirit moved in a mighty way.

At 806 N. Jefferson in Springfield, MO on Tuesday, December 22 New Life Evangelistic Center fed over 200 homeless people at the center. Then on Christmas Day 550 were fed in St. Louis at 1411 Locust. In the midst of the great financial needs NLEC was facing, God moved in a mighty way as Peter Frey from Hydromat shared $70,000. What an answer to prayer!

During 2015 we were seeing how the forces of gentrification were creating hurt, pain, and despair in the lives of the poor and homeless. Yet, during the chaos and confusion created by gentrification, I knew God was working in a mighty way. There might be trials and tribulations, but I knew that Jesus had promised He would never leave us nor forsake us. For that reason, I could face the future and whatever fiery trials it might bring.

On January 7th, 2016, New Life Evangelistic Center formally appealed to the Board of Building Appeals to overturn the decision of the Board of Public Service decision. The reasons cited for this appeal included the fact that city ordinances did not require a homeless shelter applicant to obtain the signatures of their neighbors. By requiring this "plat and petition", St. Louis was preventing a church from providing such shelter and the right to practice its religion of helping the homeless. The Board of Public Service had also ruled that NLEC had to severely limit the homeless served because they were across the street from a school. The fact was the school had gotten city permission to open across from NLEC even though the New Life church had already been providing shelter for over thirty years at that location.

Although New Life Evangelistic Center was appealing to the Board of Building Appeals, I was still skeptical of a positive decision. My skepticism was a result of the fact that the mayor had appointed each member of that board.

Even as the mayor had continued to work to shut down 1411 Locust the faithful NLEC partners who supported the work of New Life Evangelistic Center made it possible for many individuals like Annie to be helped. Annie was homeless until she came to New Life Evangelistic Center. She said, "I have slept on the sidewalk, in doorways and in abandoned buildings. I have eaten out of trashcans. I am so grateful for New Life Evangelistic Center. At New Life I have found relief, a renewed hope, and the love of God."

The pressure was increasing in the month of April, as I called upon believers in Christ to earnestly pray for New Life Evangelistic Centers work at 1411 Locust. I wrote, "To do nothing, with no other major walk-in shelters in Mid America, is to knowingly leave little children, God's precious angels, women and our homeless veterans with no place they can get into immediately in their time of need."

"Please continue to pray that God will grant strength to each one of the NLEC staff members, who are on the front lines providing for the homeless and hurting daily. Also, please pray that He will send forth His angels to assist us in this work of compassion that becomes more intense with each passing day."

Mayor Francis Slay in May 2016, boasted of having the police enforce more low-level "quality of life offenses including public urination and littering." What he didn't communicate to the public, was as he tried to appear tough on crime, this police action was directed at the homeless.

These individuals who had lost their homes were not allowed to use the bathrooms in downtown businesses, unless they made a purchase. One of the few places they could use to meet this need was the New Life Evangelistic Center at 1411 Locust. As the police were "running more warrants" on those who appeared homeless, the political power brokers and the developers were intensifying efforts to close the 1411 Locust building.

In the midst of the daily battles New Life Evangelistic Center continued to see God's faithfulness in meeting the needs of NLEC. It was June 6 that the Cahokia Family Worship Center sent a $50,000 check with a note that read, "The members of our church want to share with NLEC to help meet your many needs. We thank God for you and all Jesus has done through you in St. Louis, MO and throughout the Metro-east. May the Lord bless and keep you. May He make His face to shine upon you, and give you His perfect peace, now and always. AMEN!!"

June 16 was the date that the mayor's hand-picked Board of Building Appeals was to have made its decision concerning the shutdown of 1411 Locust. On that day, for the first time in the recent history of the St. Louis City Hall, all the electricity went off and could not be fixed. The BBA meeting was cancelled, and no date was set when a decision would be given. All of us at NLEC, along with the homeless, praised God because the 1411 Locust building would remain open, serving women and children, the elderly, veterans, and other homeless individuals.

A mayoral election was to be held in the Spring of 2017. Mayor Slay was not going to run again for re-election. He was throwing his full support behind Alderwoman Lyda Krewson. On November 3, Lauralynn Parmelee held a meet and greet in her condo with Krewson and 25 residents. At this gathering, Krewson, in an attempt to get the condo dwellers' support, declared, "NLEC has to be closed. The city should put a lock on the place."

Angie O'Gorman shared a different view on the StLToday.com website by declaring, "There are homeless on the street downtown, looking for shelter for the night. There are loft dwellers next door wining and dining with mayoral hopeful Lyda Krewson. Had Krewson taken the time to talk to the homeless too, she might have learned what caused them to be where they are and made those issues part of her mayoral run. But no, that is not Lyda Krewson. Until the causes of homelessness are effectively addressed by the City of St. Louis, every man, woman, and child who needs shelter for the night has every right to it, even if the shelter is next to a condo. The condo dwellers knew the area they were buying into. If they don't like their neighbors, they have the resources to move on. Maybe Lyda Krewson could help them do so."

New Life Evangelistic Center was issued a Cease-and-Desist Notice during the first week of November. In the days following this cease-and-desist order, someone started distributing a synthetic drug known as K2 to the homeless. Immediately New Life Evangelistic Center was blamed for the problem.

In a three-day period 44 people overdosed on the streets of St. Louis. Many of them were on Locust between 13th and 15th street. By November 12th, the number of K2 overdose cases had risen to 75.

On November 19, the St. Louis City streets department placed no parking, no stopping, and no standing signs from 14th to 15th street on Locust. Police officers were then stationed in front of 1411 Locust to see that no one stopped to drop off any type of in-kind donations including food, clothing, etc. The police wouldn't even let a lady drop off fifty sandwiches. If she wanted to leave them at 1411 Locust, she would have to park on 15th street and then carry them to the Center or call and have someone meet her there.

On November 24, Thanksgiving Day, the police were out in full force, stopping each car as they tried to unload their food in front of 1411 Locust, for the Thanksgiving dinner for the homeless. The cars were directed to 15th street where they were unloaded with volunteers helping to carry the donations a block down the streets to the 1411

Locust building.

Many volunteers for the first time were seeing that all the parking meters between 14th and 15th street on Locust had been taken out, as signs were posted by the city. These signs gave out a phone number inviting people to call if they wanted to donate. Once the number was called, the donation could then be directed to the mayor's favorite charity.

Despite these efforts to frustrate the work of the volunteers and staff at the New Life Evangelistic Center, hundreds of hurting and

Thanksgiving Dinner for the Homeless 2016

homeless people were still fed. As the dinner concluded, Elliot Davis, an anchorman on the Fox 2 news, arrived along with this daughter. Elliot had a personal Facebook following of close to 100,000 friends. When he saw how the police were standing by with orders from City Hall to stop those desiring to make donations, he did a lengthy video on his Facebook page.

Meanwhile, my associate, Ray Redlich, continued to do everything he could to convince building commissioner, Frank Oswald, to issue an occupancy permit to use 1411 Locust. The occupancy permit would be for the non-sheltering purposes of religious assembly, television studios, and general business use as the sheltering permit was pursued through the courts. NLEC building compliance manager, Jeff Schneider, would try to respond to each concern as it was brought to his attention by city inspectors. Despite these efforts, permits were still denied.

On December 29, I wrote the friends and partners of NLEC stating that, "New Life Evangelistic Center is not shutting down. Like the early Christians, who were persecuted for their faith, the staff at NLEC are now more determined than ever before to do the work of our Lord Jesus Christ.

"The enemies of the homeless may continue to lie about New Life Evangelistic Center in the media, send inspectors into the 1411 Locust building at all hours of the day and night, but we will not give up. Your NLEC will not be defeated. For God is faithful."

Chapter 7
Shut Down and Shut Out

One of the hardest things to accept is when God allows the governing powers to say, "No". That is what happened when the Board of Building Appeals said on January 12, 2017, no to New Life's appeals. They then went on to declare that NLEC had to vacate the 1411 Locust building by April 1.

Lauralynn Parmelee was quickly becoming a face of the gentrifiers who wanted to shut down 1411 Locust and drive the homeless out of the neighborhood. She had joined Laura Griffin and Matthew O'Leary in incorporating the Neighborhood Improvement Association, Downtown West.

Lauralynn in an email blast to 30 people, including Mayor Francis Slay had this to say about the homeless, "I have a BB gun and I am going to go out and start shooting those people in the ass," if the city didn't padlock New Life. She went on to say, "go ahead and arrest me. Jail will be quieter than here."

Then she continued to say in her email, "I just looked out the window and there is a van full of students from St. Louis University mixing with the crowd. Maybe I should shoot them too."

The homeless that Lauralynn Parmalee, Brad Waldrop, Laura Griffin, Matt O'Leary and others supporting their efforts of gentrification were attacking were human beings. These were people made in the image of God.

March 12 in my journal I wrote, "I'm trying to avoid a meltdown but dear God to be honest I'm starting to panic. Two and a half weeks from Saturday is April 1. Now the city of St. Louis wants to shut the New Life Evangelistic Center at 1411 Locust down. The police seem to have a plan in place. One officer had even picked up Pattie on the street. After she told him that she was staying at 1411 Locust the officer insisted on dropping her off at the Gateway 180 shelter. When she went to the door, the shelter told her they had no room and she had to walk back to 1411 Locust. The captain of the Police force refuses to meet with Rev. Ray. The captain told Ray conversations had to be with the city counselor."

New Life Evangelistic Center in the days that followed filed a motion in Judge Moriarity's City Circuit Court to stop the Board of Building Appeals decision. The intent of this motion was to get the judge to issue an order to stop the April 1st shut down.

The St. Louis Affordable Housing Commission had earlier in the month approved $214,000 for shelter for some of the people that would be back out on the streets when the city closed 1411 Locust. Since 1976 New Life had faithfully assisted the homeless at 1411 Locust without using any funds from taxpayers. Now in addition to the hundreds of thousands of dollars the city had spent on legal expenses to shut down 1411 Locust, it was having to spend even more to shelter the homeless that NLEC had been providing for without taxpayer funding.

On March 30, St. Louis Circuit Court Judge Joan Moriarity denied NLEC's request for a stay. She had accepted the city's statement that they would provide for the homeless. Without investigating Judge Moriarity declared in her order March 30, "Evidence was produced at the hearing that there is now available in the city of St. Louis facilities with sufficient bed space to house homeless men, women and children who would be displaced due to the closing of the New Life Evangelistic Center. The evidence further indicates that these facilities are all in compliance with St. Louis City Code. Therefore, it is ordered and decreed that Plaintiff New Life Evangelistic Center, Inc.'s Motion for stay is hereby denied."

The Arch City Defender's and the legal clinic at St. Louis University on March 31 knowing the city did not have adequate shelter for those being put out of NLEC, proceeded to sue the City of St. Louis.

How I thank God for those who have the courage to stand up to injustice. Anthony Shahid is such a person. He would declare at the rallies, "the reason Larry Rice is having so many direct attacks by City Hall is that he refuses to be Francis Slay's boy."

The clock was ticking, and we only had a matter of hours before the shut down was to take place at 5 pm April 2 at 1411 Locust. On Saturday, April 1, the day before the hour of destruction, as NLEC staff were busy moving the Television Studio to 2428 Woodson Road in Overland, along with the development office and printing department, a rally was held at 10 am at 1411 Locust. It was an encouragement to hear from so many people whose lives had been changed because of NLEC's work at 1411 Locust. That night I went to the various areas in the building where the homeless were staying and said my goodbyes. I had to admit it was one of the hardest and saddest nights of my life.

The next day April 2 another rally was held at 2 pm. Once again numerous testimonies were given by individuals whose lives have been impacted by the work of NLEC. One was given by University City Councilman, Ron, who told how God used NLEC to change his life. Another testimony was by a woman who was a former prostitute who had been saved at NLEC. Ellie Rice, my own granddaughter also gave a very moving statement.

As 5:00 p.m. arrived, the staff of New Life Evangelistic Center and the homeless remaining went peaceably outside the building. Judy Redlich shared the following from her perspective of what the exit was like:

"Closing time came at 5:00 p.m., Sunday evening April 2, just as the city said. They put a cease-and-desist sign on the front door of the New Life Evangelistic Center. The police then began their search of the building. Ray and I worked together packing up the important things in Ray's office. As we packed, we had no idea if anyone would be permitted to even come into the building to work. So, we packed his telephone, his computer, and other items he felt he might need as he would have to set up a new office.

"At 5:00 p.m., I came out of the back of the building through the tunnel right behind Debra Rice. It was very narrow, but we made it through."

"I remembered 45 years before when the 1411 Locust building was first opened. I remember standing on the roof of the building on a sunny spring day. Along with the NLEC board members we prayed believing God to provide the money to purchase this majestic 5 story building in the heart of downtown St. Louis. Both KNLC TV 24 was housed there along with the shelter for the growing homeless population."

"This night would be the first night in the building's history that the doors would be locked. Someone was always in the building, and I don't even know if they had a key to the front door. As I recalled, the back door going out to the gated parking area was never locked. The only thing that locks is the back gate that cuts the back of the property off from the alley behind."

"Then my husband, Ray Redlich came out and got into the car. We drove around the front of the building one last time before heading home. Demonstrators were there standing in solidarity with the police keeping the peace."

The night of April 2, I spent outside with the homeless. Joining me in sleeping outside of 1411 Locust were Mark, Phil, Dan, my grand-daughter Elle Rice, and others. We had a chance to minister throughout the night to the homeless who came to the doors of 1411 Locust for shelter, blankets, care kits and water.

Ray Redlich shared that, "In the wake of the anti-homeless sweep on April 3, the day after the closing of 1411 Locust, my heart was sickened even more to see some of the same city officials and attorneys who had opposed New Life Evangelistic Center during the previous three years now walking up and down the street exulting in their victory. It looked to me like a party — a victory celebration. After all, they had accomplished their objective. The last major walk-in shelter in the St. Louis region was now closed."

"Nobody who truly cared about the homeless celebrated, however. During the ensuing days numerous people came by – expecting to receive help or to offer help – only to discover that this fine five-story building that had served the community for 45 years was now closed."

The next day, April 4, the day of the election, New Life Evangelistic Center received a notice from building inspector, Paul Wood, that the house the women and children had moved to at 5811 Michigan had been condemned. The condemnation order said these women were there illegally and there was no permit for the facility. Later after our attorney Todd Lubben contacted the city attorney's office, it was de-

termined that NLEC had gathered signatures from surrounding neighbor's years earlier and made application for a shelter. The signatures and application had been misplaced at City Hall. The condemnation case was not pursued further by the city, and the women and children remained.

Lyda Krewson won the election, and I knew the gentrification policies of the Slay Administration would remain in effect.

The days following, I found myself battling depression. I was feeling very broken over the shutdown of the shelter, the election of Lyda Krewson who wanted a lock on 1411 Locust, and the cities aggressive anti-homeless policies which had extended to the attempted condemnation of 5811 Michigan. It was so hard to keep on going.

It wasn't until an awards ceremony the evening of April 7 that I started feeling the healing take place. This awards ceremony was sponsored by a dynamic youth organization that Anthony Shahid directed. The encouragement from the people attending was really uplifting to me personally.

During the days leading up to Easter, I found myself having to release so many things into the hands of God. My hope for the future was centered on the resurrection of Jesus Christ. I knew that the forces of evil might shut down a building, but they could not shut down a church.

The NLEC staff that had been living at 1411 Locust were transferred to the houses on Michigan Streets. Men went to our training centers in New Bloomfield and to the parsonage at Transformation Church. How I thanked God for the fact that Chris and Martha had relocated to Marshfield months earlier. Now they were able to direct the staff who were being sent to that location.

A three-bedroom house was rented next to 2428 Woodson in Overland where television and renewable energy personnel were able to live. Pastor Mark Glenn who was on the

HOTS – Help on the Streets event at City Hall in St. Louis City

NLEC staff in Overland took over many of Pastor Ray Redlich's responsibilities. This freed Ray and other staff members to dedicate themselves to helping the homeless on the streets of St. Louis.

I also decided that it was important to host once a week a bus ticket distribution event under Mayor Krewson's window on Market Street. The first was held on Good Friday morning. Surveys were taken from among the homeless people attending the first two events from which we learned the following:

83

Women signing up to receive Bus Tickets

After surveying 157 homeless men and women we discovered over 70% of the homeless stated they were staying at New Life before it closed.

Over 65% said they had been harassed by Police since NLEC closed. Many of these persons found it hypocritical when the same police who directed them to sleep on the sidewalks adjacent to New Life while it was open – were now ordering them away from NLEC upon its closure.

About 50% of the homeless were spending the nights at the Biddle House, the Weed Control Storage Facility and Garage, and the 12th and Park Rec Center. The other 50% had nowhere to sleep.

Ray described his daily work now among the homeless in downtown St. Louis by saying, "Since the closing of New Life, our mission of aid has taken us literally to the streets of Saint Louis City. We discovered many of the homeless – unable to find shelter – sleeping behind dumpsters, in the parks or wherever they could. There were still many others who were forced to flee to vacos (vacant houses or buildings). Often these vacos offered little comfort or security since these structures were usually condemned with no running water, electricity or gas."

Despite the determination of the enemies of the homeless to shut down the work of New Life Evangelistic Center the Spirit of God continued to move. As New Life team members went to the streets of downtown St. Louis serving the homeless, they saw the critical need that existed for transportation assistance. As a result, the number of bus tickets given out each week skyrocketed.

Individuals like Shay would report, "I was robbed at gunpoint this month after I got my disability check, and the robber took all my money."

"I am hoping to find a place to live. The bus tickets that New Life Evangelistic Center gave me made it possible for me to go to different apartment buildings and apply for a place to stay. I have degenerative disc disease in my back, so it is very hard for me to walk long distances, as a result the bus tickets are a great help to me."

Crystal reported that, "I know that I can keep my children out of the rain and off the streets on a bus if I have to with these tickets."

Sharonne testified how the bus tickets helped her to get to work and see her teenage children. Without the bus tickets she said, "I wouldn't be able to see my children and would lose my job." Each week the amount of money NLEC was spending with Bi-State continued to raise.

Since my son Chris and his wife, Martha were in Marshfield, they could assist the trainees and Chris could also assist Joe Batson in Springfield. At the NLEC's Veterans Coming Home Center at 806 N. Jefferson in Springfield, Missouri New Life was assisting the homeless with meals, clothing, showers, computer service, a place to store their belongings, rest, and laundry facilities. The homeless were also given the opportunity to be set free from the cycle of homeless through New Life's residential training programs.

Martha and Chris were assisted in Marshfield by Eddie, Benny and Joyce, along with Angela who had been in the training program in St. Louis. Other homeless individuals and married couples like Stella and Levi would come to train under the direction of Chris and Martha in Marshfield. At that location they could participate in renewable energy fairs, a farm with a dairy cow and calf, goats, sheep, a free store and a radio station.

Stella and Levi were alive because a caring State Trooper in Illinois had stopped them from committing suicide and had gotten them into a hospital for treatment.

When they were released from the hospital with nowhere to go, they were once again sleeping outside. Then they met the NLEC outreach

Levi and Stella, December 2017

team in downtown St. Louis. Stella and Levi had been told that bus tickets, with emergency supplies were given away by New Life every Friday morning under the mayor's window outside St. Louis city hall. After attending that event, Stella and Levi decided to get involved in the NLEC training program. Within a matter of days, they were in Marshfield, Missouri. At that location they continued to grow in the grace of God as they developed a wide range of skills that have enabled them to help the homeless both in Marshfield and Springfield.

Joe Batson, who coordinated New Life's work in Springfield, Missouri would receive additional help from Joe, John, Homer, and others who were previously in the NLEC Leadership Training Program at 1411 Locust in St. Louis. Other NLEC program staff went to New Bloomfield, Potosi, Joplin and Van Buren.

In New Bloomfield the training opportunities for the previously homeless would expand from the Here's Help Radio Network and Renewable Energy to also include New Life's Charolais Cattle Farms.

The largest growth in the work of New Life Evangelistic Center, following the closing of 1411 Locust, took place in St. Louis County. With the headquarters of the New Life Evangelistic Center now moved to 2428 Woodson Road in Overland, Missouri, those desiring to be a part of the TV, Renewable Energy, Development or the NLEC Energy Assistance programs now found opportunities to serve God at this new headquarters.

The financial crisis continued to grow at NLEC as it worked to acquire housing for the staff and trainees, meet the legal expenses, along with providing bus passes, utility assistance and other emergency needs for the poor and homeless.

It had appeared for months, that in addition to trying to shut down New Life Evangelistic Center through the legal process, the enemies of New Life's work among the homeless were trying to do everything they could to shut down New Life financially. This included trying to destroy New Life Evangelistic Center's reputation in the community through the media as well as using the police to make it difficult for donors to bring donations to 1411 Locust.

As I joined the NLEC staff in earnestly praying daily for the financial needs, we would continue to see one miracle after another performed through caring people who loved God and His homeless people. Even with these series of miracles the "red ink" continued to flow. The bills due had grown to over $400,000.

As I cried out to the Lord, He began to show me how the viewing habits of growing numbers of people were changing. Instead of just watching conventional television programs provided by over the air television stations more and more people were turning to social media and apps on mobile devices. If this trend continued, within a matter of years UHF Channel 24 TV could be worth very little. As this took place, major work also needed to take place on both the KNLC TV 24 transmitter and tower.

Earlier in the year through a miraculous chain of events, I had met Kyle Walker. He was an executive with Weigel Broadcasting. This was the group that owned Memory TV or Me TV, presently broadcast on 4.2. It consisted of classical TV shows, many of which we had ran throughout the years on KNLC TV 24.

I knew if we were to consider selling KNLC TV, Weigel Broadcasting would have to let NLEC continue to use 24.2 and allow New Life to keep the smaller KNLC tower on which we had a FM radio antenna plus other clients. In addition, New Life Evangelistic Center needed to continue to own all the acreage NLEC presently had in House Springs.

Weigel Broadcasting would have to agree to these terms plus give New Life Evangelistic Center three million, seven hundred and fifty thousand dollars for KNLC TV 24. This would allow New Life to pay off all its bills, loans, make repairs on all NLEC facilities, expand New Life's mission work in India and acquire Safe Houses for homeless women and children.

The sale of TV 24 would make it possible for NLEC to have additional resources to directly help the poor and homeless with bus tickets, energy assistance, housing placement and other emergency needs. It would permit NLEC to have a legal reserve fund along with the resources to acquire staff housing facilities at various locations and make the improvements required to get back into 1411 Locust.

Before the summer ended, both Weigel Broadcasting and the New Life Evangelistic Center Board had come to an agreement. The application to transfer the ownership of KNLC was then made to the Federal Communications Commission. Once that happened, Charlie Hale, Jeannette Carrington and the NLEC Tech Team went to work creating an app for NLEC TV. The television crew presently on site in House Springs continued to live at that site preparing to broadcast on NLEC TV 24.2 like they had done on TV 24.1.

When the sale was announced to the public, I was quoted in the St. Louis Post Dispatch as saying, "Given the drastic cutbacks in state funding, if we didn't make this move at this time, there would be tremendous human suffering on the streets. With the shelter closed, we must find (homeless) people housing, and that costs more money than having them stay at the Locust shelter."

As negotiations concerning the sale of KNLC were taking place, New Life Evangelistic Center continued to make repairs at 1411 Locust in response to citations from St. Louis inspectors. We had been led to believe that if we made these repairs, New Life Evangelistic Center could reopen as a church and provide basic day services to the homeless, as we went through the legal process to reopen as a shelter.

Despite all the repairs being made, the St. Louis Building Commissioner, Frank Oswald, continued to give NLEC the run around. When Ray Redlich asked him what additional specific repairs would be needed to obtain an occupancy permit. Ray could never get a straight answer.

As this took place, life was becoming increasingly difficult for the homeless who were trying to survive on the "streets" of St. Louis. The auxiliary men's shelter the city had provided was closed. The city's women's shelter at 12th and Park ceased to operate. All that remained was the Biddle House for men.

Increasing numbers of the homeless were starting to live in vacant buildings known on the street as "vacos". Often this act of desperation resulted in the homeless becoming victims of violence. Such was the case of Natasha, who was violently attacked as she slept in the abandoned Carr School building. In that vacant building, Natasha was severely beaten with a hammer along with John, Andrea and Will.

Following that attack I pleaded with churches to open their doors, in order that New Life Evangelistic Center could work with them to provide shelter for the homeless women and children. I was quoted on KMOX radio saying, "We'd be happy to meet with them (churches), help them get the necessary cots and blankets and provide volunteers. My pitch to them (the pastors) is this: we've got to start not just talking the talk but walking the walk."

The need among the homeless women was critical. For example, there was Rhonda, who after being stranded in St. Louis for 4 months, and being robbed of her money and ID, had nowhere to go. The grass lawn at a downtown Casino was her bed. Rhonda needed a place to take a shower and other help that she couldn't find. She needed a safe place to sleep. She couldn't get a cell phone or food stamps because she has no address to send mail to and no ID because hers was stolen.

The first NLEC Safe House opened in St. Louis on Michigan Blvd.

The center accommodated women and children. Within a short period of time after it opened, the center saw miracles unfold in the lives of hurting women like Laura. Laura said, "I became homeless on May 23, 2017, when the brokerage company I had paid rent to for years suddenly refused to take anymore payments from me unless I paid them in cash. When I wouldn't, they refused to accept my rent. I was threatened with a lawsuit unless I vacated the premises by May 24, 2017."

"So, I moved my things out of the apartment and looked for a shelter or somewhere I could go. There was nowhere for me to go. I met Rev. Larry Rice and the New Life Evangelistic Center staff at an event downtown where they were giving away bus tickets and supplies to those living on the streets. I then came home to the New Life Safe House. Since I have been there, I have found love and support from the other women and children at the center."

Laura – May, 2017

I thanked God we were able to help these women, but this was only a drop in the vast ocean of need. At this point it would have been so easy to simply be depressed over all the unmet needs around me. Instead, I chose to ask myself what the Psalmist did in Psalm 42, verse 5 and verse 11 and Psalm 43:5, "Why are you cast down, O my soul, and why are you in turmoil within me? Hope in God; for I shall again praise him, my salvation and my God."

On August 10 I wrote in my journal, "The architectural plans were turned into the city for 1411 Locust today. I believe God is not only desiring to fix up the building, but He also wants to do improvements inside of me. My anxious thoughts and worries about the future and a multitude of other fears and resentments must be surrendered so I can become a new creation in Christ. I have so many concerns, when my main concern should involve totally surrendering all to Christ. As I journey through the Bible, reading it book by book, I am presently studying Joshua, Ecclesiastes, Ezekiel and I Thessalonians. I pray that I may gain the Biblical principles needed to see a Christ-like change in my life. Today over one hundred and twenty-five homeless people were helped in front of City Hall."

Chapter 8
Following Jesus into the Hurting and Suffering of the Homeless

With the arrival of winter, the NLEC staff and myself found ourselves following Jesus into the suffering of the homeless women who were being left on the streets of St. Louis. I expressed this in a letter that was sent to our NLEC partners in November of 2017. I wrote, "Please help relieve the panic of having nowhere to go by helping me provide a home for the many mothers and children who are homeless. Shay is one of those who need help now. Shay says, 'I called all the different contact numbers to find my husband and myself shelter. One place we were referred to wasn't even open yet. They were still working on restoring their building.'

"The closing of New Life Evangelistic Center was bad. Just very bad. Now there is no food, no shelter, no safety. Even the police who are supposed to serve and protect us said they don't want us down here. So where are we supposed to go? My husband and I scraped and saved to buy our own tent. This is our new home now. It keeps us warm. Protects us from the rain, sleet and snow. But it mostly keeps us together. Now the city says we can't even be in our tent. Please help New Life so they can help us."

I continued in my letter to the donors of New Life Evangelistic Center, "We need to open a four-bedroom house immediately. As we use this to respond to emergency situations, we will work to complete the repairs at 1411 Locust. The women and children must have a place to stay this winter."

As the first winter since the closing of 1411 Locust set in, the reality that New Life Evangelistic Center would not be back in 1411 Locust for Thanksgiving was beginning to hit me hard. For forty-five years the homeless, fatherless, and elderly were able to gather for not only a great meal but a time of fellowship with individuals from all walks of life. Needs were not only met in the lives of the poor and elderly at these Thanksgiving celebrations, but caring people were able to express the love and compassion they felt by being waiters, waitresses, hosts, kitchen helpers, drivers and more.

As I prayed with the New Life team it became clear that we needed to hold the Thanksgiving Dinner outside this year in the street in front of 1411 Locust. While the NLEC staff made plans for Thanksgiving, on November 16th my son Chris and I took a homeless couple who were stranded in Springfield, to their family in Rose Bud, Texas. The next day I described in my journal the events that followed. "Today Chris and I visited the First Baptist Church in Sutherland Springs, Texas. It was at this church that on November 5 a gunman walked into the church and killed twenty-six members and wounded twenty others. After reading about their food bank days earlier, we had felt led by God to give a check of $500 to the new directors of this food pantry, Rod and Judy Green. They were determined to continue this outreach after their co-worker Lula White was killed November 5."

"As I talked with Rod, who was an elder at the First Baptist Church, it became clear that both of our congregations had been directly attacked by Satan in an attempt to destroy our ministries. Rod related to me how his church was determined to continue serving God even though two-thirds of the congregation had been killed or wounded."

I knew that despite the attacks we had to maintain the same kind of commitment at the New Life Evangelistic Center. For that reason, two days later I wrote the following Thanksgiving Day letter to the homeless, "This Thanksgiving we are celebrating our 45th Annual Thanksgiving Dinner on the streets because we are homeless like many of you. As you know, New Life Evangelistic Center has been driven from its home at 1411 Locust because of gentrification.

"Gentrification is such a wicked thing – Amos, Micah, Isaiah and other Old Testament prophets spoke out against it. Gentrification is progress at the expense of the poor and homeless. The wickedness of gentrification can be clearly seen at 1411 Locust in St. Louis. This five-story building is forced to remain closed as homeless people wander the streets all night in search of a place to sleep."

Thanksgiving, 2017

93

Thanksgiving, 2017

God blessed that Thanksgiving Dinner in a mighty way. As the New Life team followed Jesus into the pain of the homeless, two food trucks were used to provide over 400 dinners to the hungry and homeless. A great multitude of volunteers from throughout the Bi-State area also assisted.

While the hungry were being provided for in downtown St. Louis over two hundred homeless people were being fed at the NLEC Veterans Coming Home Center in Springfield, Missouri. What a blessing it was to have

so many provided for. Jeff, a homeless man told KY3 TV, "The people helping, I think they're great. They're being led by the Spirit of God to help the less fortunate out. The people coming in to eat, these people have been through a lot. Their circumstances may vary one after the other, but they're all human beings and deserve to be treated as such with decency, respect, dignity and all."

The shutdown of 1411 Locust was devastating to Grover. In the days that followed he would stumble through each day trying to survive. Grover started drinking more to deaden the pain. Finally, in October Grover was sick and tired of being told by the police and the security guards in downtown businesses that he couldn't sit or sleep where his weary body collapsed. He decided to make the port-a-potty on North Seventh Street in downtown St. Louis his home. After moving into the port-a-potty there were times when Grover felt so alone that he would just yell to hear his own voice. Other times Grover would play music on the radio he carried with him.

As time passed, Grover was getting lonelier and lonelier and started drinking more. It was then that as he screamed louder and louder, he descended further into the dark abyss of depression.

December had arrived and as the nights got colder it was becoming harder for the 56-year-old Grover Perry. He had been in a special education program and even later trained to do auto body repair. Now Grover felt totally alone.

But Grover was not alone when it came to suffering. Jesus was there with him and the hundreds of homeless people who were struggling to survive in the winter of 2017-2018 in downtown St. Louis.

The NLEC architect had tried to satisfy the St. Louis Building Commissioner to the extent he had resubmitted drawings on October 6, November 1, November 8 and November 20. Instead of approving the drawings, Frank Oswald sent Ray Redlich a two-and-a-half-page letter on December 4 continuing to drag out the permitting process.

I wrote on December 11 that the St. Louis area is made up of 2 cities. "The first consists of those with warm homes who have money, power and influence. The second city is made up of the poor, the elderly and the homeless. I call this city number two where the struggle for daily survival consumes the thoughts and preoccupations of these citizens."

It was this city number two that Grover Perry lived in until Wednesday, December 20. On that day someone noticed the door to the grey porta-potty that was Grover's home was cracked open. At around noon as employees at a nearby Christmas office party were gorging themselves on roast beef and turkey, the police arrived and found Grover dead in his porta-potty home. It was then they transported his body to the morgue.

Following Jesus into the pain and suffering of the homeless that Christmas meant burying Grover and buying safe houses for the homeless women.

Christmas at
Transformation Christian

On Christmas Day Transformation Christian Church allowed New Life Evangelistic Center to use its Family Life Center for the NLEC Christmas party. The homeless were picked up from in front of 1411 Locust and brought to the church. There, they were greeted by a host of volunteers from Transformation as well as others from throughout the bi-state area. The homeless were treated to a large Christmas dinner with a wide range of Christmas gifts including Bi-State Bus Tickets given to them.

It was the miracle of God's love demonstrated through the sending of His Son, which gave me the strength to move into the New Year of 2018. On New Year's Day, January 1, 2018, tragedy struck once again. The body of a 54-year-old man was found in a dumpster located in the 2000 block of Madison Street. No matter how hard the winter patrol teams worked the previous night this man still died from hypothermia as he slept in a dumpster. Firefighters who were responding to a call in the area were told, "there was a body inside the trash bin".

As the temperature continued to drop and people were dying, attorney Elkin Kistner, on behalf of his clients at 1426 Washington Ave. and the Neighborhood Improvement Association Downtown West filed a new lawsuit naming the City of St. Louis and NLEC as defendants. These groups were petitioning the Court to find that the City could not issue an occupancy permit for a day shelter because the City was applying incorrect codes. It was obvious that the purpose of the suit was to see to it that New Life Evangelistic Center remained closed and the homeless kept out of the neighborhood.

Many of the homeless would have died during the winter of 2018 if churches like Transformation, St. Peter AME, Destiny Family Church and others would not have opened their doors and provided shelter. Even as these ministries extended hospitality to the hurting and homeless many felt the Krewson administration was ignoring the homeless epidemic.

Even with one attack after another New Life Evangelistic Center continued to intensify its services in the winter of 2017-2018. NLEC placed the homeless into motels, in apartments and given transportation assistance to go to their families in other states. These included Becky, who was living on the streets for three years until NLEC got her back with her family in Des Moines, Iowa. Susan who had throat cancer was put into an apartment of her own because of New Life's assistance.

In the days that followed the generosity of caring individuals made it possible for NLEC to acquire a four-bedroom home to be used as a safe house. Now previously homeless women like Angela and Linda not only had a home they could stay in, but they would also provide for other homeless women like Candice.

New Life Evangelistic Center was able to follow Jesus daily into the pain of the hurting and homeless because of its dedicated team of donors, prayer warriors, and staff members. The monies that New Life Evangelistic Center had received as a result of the sale of KNLC TV was quickly being used up. After all the 2017 bills were paid, loans repaid, buildings repaired, and staff quarters acquired these resources were almost depleted.

For that reason, the daily gifts of caring people along with individuals like Ronald Butler, who remembered New Life Evangelistic Center in their wills, were miracles directly from heaven. The money Ronald left New Life Evangelistic Center in two bank accounts enabled NLEC to help the poor and elderly with their utility bills, provide direct assistance to the homeless and continue to help New Life remain current in meeting its financial obligations. I could not help but praise God for His faithfulness as He miraculously met the needs of New Life Evangelistic Center each and every day.

Only God knows how many of the homeless, who were part of the New Life Evangelistic Center family congregation died during the winter of 2017-2018! After the deaths in December and January were reported the city of St. Louis went to great lengths to see that the deaths of additional homeless people were not made available to the media.

After the closing of the overnight shelter and day center at 1411 Locust on April 2, 2017, the homeless in downtown St. Louis had become increasingly desperate.

The desperation became clear March 6, 2018, when Paul Barroni, after being turned down for a bed at Biddle House, went to Clayton to carry out a robbery at C.J. Mugg's. He had one goal in mind. That goal was to return to prison, so he would have a place to sleep, food to eat and the opportunity to shower regularly.

Paul had walked into the bar with his finger under his coat to look like a gun was hidden there. After the bartender handed him a stack of bills and a roll of quarters, Paul ordered her to call the police.

Later Barroni told detectives he robbed the bar, so he could return to prison because he didn't want to be homeless.

Homeless individuals would regularly join the New Life Staff in holding up signs protesting gentrification in downtown St. Louis as they distributed literature. In the meantime, the NLEC legal team continued to move through the state courts. On August 1, Todd Lubben appeared before the Missouri Court of Appeals on behalf of New Life Evangelistic Center.

In his appeal Todd responded to Confluence Academy School's attempt to reverse both the Board of Building Appeals and the Circuit Court's decision that the Academy's location across from 1411 Locust should stop NLEC from having a shelter there.

Confluence Academy, although it established its school several years after NLEC was assisting the homeless, still wanted the shelter closed in order to isolate its students from the homeless.

When I saw the order from the Missouri Court of Appeals, on September 26, 2018, I must admit I was shocked at the position the court took. I was surprised the court did not realize the tremendous effort New Life Evangelistic Center had made, to get signatures from its neighbors granting it permission to continue operating its shelter at 1411 Locust.

Mark Glenn, Ray Redlich, and teams of volunteers had tried to get into the condominium building at 15th and Locust to get signatures from the residents inside. The management of the facility had refused NLEC workers the right of entry. As a result, for days, efforts were made to approach individuals rushing in and out of the building.

Even though these efforts were made, it was obvious that the Missouri Court of Appeals did not understand this, by the conclusions it drew.

For New Life Evangelistic Center, giving up was not an option. The NLEC first responders continued to help the homeless daily. These hurting individuals included Brandy, who Ray and the NLEC team found in a vacant building at 13th and Cass. Brandy, after falling into a fire, was severely burned. When she was found in that vacant building the evening of September 29, 2018, Ray rushed her to the hospital where she was immediately admitted and treated for her burns.

As the needs among the homeless and hurting continued in 2018, I also was encountering a series of personal losses. Lee, who had been arrested with me during an act of civil disobedience (see Chapter 5) was found dead in his car in Belleville. Earlier in the year Barbara Martin, who was the nurse for the homeless at 1411 Locust, for over 20 years, died on February 7. Then on February 25 my 10-year-old grandson Henry First died. On Friday, April 13, my longtime associate and good friend Jim Barnes went to be with Jesus. Jim was the man God had used to build KNLC Channel 24 and the Here's Help Radio and TV Network.

I continued to grieve every time one of my homeless friends died in the vacant houses or wherever they could find a place to lay their heads. This included "Midnight" as he was found shot to death in the street near the vacant house he lived in.

It was all happening at once. Death, loss and growing despair in the lives of the homeless. At this same time gentrifiers continued to push in the courts a lawsuit to keep the city of St. Louis from issuing New Life permits for daytime services. As Hosea 10:4 says, "Lawsuit's spring up like poisonous weeds in a plowed field."

As the New Life staff followed Jesus into the suffering of the homeless we asked them how they continued to have hope in spite of their homelessness. Andre, who had been on the streets for weeks said, "Hope helps me keep my sanity." Ericka, who was "couch surfing" between family and friends says, "Hope is all I have to keep me sane and not cry."

Priscilla wrote, "Being homeless is a struggle. It involves looking for work without means. Having no money for the bus as you sleep on the floors and try to get one meal a day. But in spite of the circumstances, I have hope for the future because God says in Jeremiah 29:11, "For I know the plans I have for you," declares the Lord, "plans to prosper you and not to harm you, plans to give you hope and a future."

Denni admitted she didn't have much hope and could barely smile. Ashley, who was sleeping on the streets by churches and in parks said, "You have to have faith to keep going." As Jennifer slept in an abandoned building, she said that hope, "is the only thing that keeps me going."

Markus, who had been sleeping on bus stop benches for five weeks said, "Hope and faith helps me get through each day. If I keep my faith, I know things will get better." Community activist, Zaki Baruti said, "Keeping hope alive involves a strong belief in God and the subsequent work that is needed to actualize the aspiration."

The closing of 1411 Locust did not stop New Life Evangelistic Center from its work of providing hope to the homeless. One of the ways of doing this was to open safe houses throughout the Bi-State area.

Rachael Rice described what the safe houses meant to Sanita, Terry, and other homeless women. Her article entitled, "Last Resort", was published in the St. Louis Post Dispatch October 3, 2018.

The article profiled several women staying at NLEC safe houses. It described how they called the St. Louis homeless hotline every day asking for bed space in area shelters and how they were denied. While at the safe houses they applied for jobs and watched the children that were too young for school.

In November and December of 2018 New Life provided further hope to the homeless by adding two additional safe houses. One was for the women and children and the second was for the homeless veterans. This brought the total to four safe houses for the women and two for the homeless veterans.

The provision of the safe houses, the transportation assistance, NLEC training programs and the many other ways New Life Evangelistic Center provided help to the homeless trying to survive outside did not slow down our efforts to get back into 1411 Locust. The reopening of this facility was critical for not only helping the homeless survive physically as winter approached but also spiritually.

Warren, who had nowhere but the "streets" (as the homeless called it), said that the "sermons I received at 1411 Locust kept me focused. The streets are mean. At New Life we were treated with respect." Jason who also now sleeps on the "streets" said of 1411 Locust, "I could get together with my

Christian brothers and sisters."

"My faith is important to me. It keeps me strong, and I feel motivated because I do believe in Jesus." Allen writes. "1411 Locust was a place for us to stay. I enjoyed the Bible Studies. They helped me grow in my faith."

Working to keep hope alive for those left on the streets without a place to call home, NLEC challenged the Bi-State area to get involved in Socktober. This was an all-out effort in October to gather winter socks, care kits, insulated underwear, blankets, sleeping bags, and anything and everything the homeless would need to survive outside this winter. This effort continued into November and December with special events for the homeless taking place at Thanksgiving and Christmas.

As the court battles continued to take place, I remembered the words of Winston Churchill who said during the Nazi bombings, "Success is moving from one failure to another with no loss of enthusiasm."

A call for prayer was issued to reopen 1411 Locust as we continued to move forth with enthusiasm. This call for prayer also included asking God to move on churches that winter to open their doors to provide shelter to those sleeping outside.

With each day that passed, as 1411 locust remained closed, I knew growing numbers of men, women and children were suffering as they tried to survive outdoors. Yet, I also knew that getting bitter over this injustice would not solve anything. I had to let the love of Christ flow in the very essence of my being as I followed Jesus offering direct help, into the pain of the hurting and homeless.

In order to help me do that I have to remember the words of Archbishop Oscar Romero who said prior to his death by an assassin's bullet, "Don't be led astray either by the allure of power and money or by following false ideologies. True hope is not found there either. True hope is not found in a revolution of violence and bloodshed, and hope is not found in money and power – neither on the left nor on the right. The hope that we must account for and that makes us speak with valor is found in Christ, who reigns after death, even after murderous death. And with Him reign all who have preached His justice, His hope, and His peace."

With this fact in mind, I know we can keep hope alive, as we follow Jesus into the pain, suffering and injustice of the homeless.

Chapter 9
Sharing God's Faithfulness and Love in the Midst of Suffering

Jesus was very explicit about what He wanted his followers to do when it came to feeding the hungry, sheltering the homeless and helping those in need. In Matthew 25:31-46 Jesus said as often as we did it for "the least of these" even so, we have done it for Him. The problem is this will often bring the followers of Christ into direct opposition to local municipalities who will do everything they can to shut down the work of God. They do this if they cannot control it and use that ministry for their own political purposes.

Ray Redlich

On Halloween, 2018, St. Louis Police gave Ray Redlich and Christopher Ohnimus a ticket for giving sandwiches to the homeless. Although the case was later dropped, the Freedom Center of Missouri, on behalf of Ray and Christopher filed a lawsuit against the city. The attorney who was representing them pro-bono was David Roland. He said, "The 11th Circuit Court of Appeals ruled that sharing food with the needy is itself an act of expressive conduct. It is protected by the First Amendment. It is one of the bedrock ideas of Christianity, and in fact the Bible says that in giving food to even the least of these, you are giving food to Jesus Himself. That is why it is so crucial to these gentlemen's faith."

The Riverfront Times reported that the citation violated Ray and Christopher's "right to practice their religion." The lawsuit also alleged the citation violated "their freedom of expression, their freedom of association, and their right of conscience", the Post-Dispatch reported.

"I call it ministering to people," Ray said to KMOX radio. "That means serving. We are ministering to the people on the streets, both spiritually and materially.

St. Louis Public Radio reported that in the lawsuit the two men say it is an "obligation as a follower of Jesus Christ to feed the hungry. It is unconstitutional to apply the regulations to people who are feeding others for religious reasons, instead of for profit."

In addition to feeding the hungry, New Life Evangelistic Center continued to shelter the homeless and reunite families through its Safe Houses, Residential Training Centers, and placing previously homeless families into a home of their own.

Quinsota Boyd had to separate from his wife and children because of their homelessness. This changed after they were placed in a home that New Life Evangelistic Center had purchased in Cahokia, Illinois. At first, the couple made monthly payments for a year then New Life forgave the remaining money owed and gave the family the title to the house.

The Boyd Family in front of their home.

After seeing the house for the first time, Quinsota called it, "the first day of the rest of their lives".

For nine months he and his family had slept on the streets. Quinsota said, "We became homeless due to financial struggles and stuff like that." He explained why he had to separate from his family, "Sanita (his wife) and the children were sleeping in the shelters for women and children, while I slept outside. It was something we had to do for the situation we were in."

"As of today, we have a new address and a new home. It is really a blessing." Quinsota said their re-union in a home of their own wouldn't have been possible without New Life Evangelistic Center. "You can have peace when you know you have a home and a family to come home to. It's a beautiful life and I got a beautiful wife and children".

In December of 2018, the Holy Spirit began to deal heavily with me concerning approaching my grandson Chris Aaron about coming to work at NLEC and begin learning how to direct New Life Evangelistic Center in the future. Chris Aaron described his response to this invitation, and his first year of training in 2019, in the following way.

"My grandfather called me one day and asked me to pray about joining New Life Evangelistic Center in a leadership position. He had never approached me before in such a way, and I felt the Holy Spirit in the conversation. There have only been a few moments like that in my life, where I could feel God's Spirit weighing heavily on the conversation. After the phone call, my spirit was not at rest. Day after day I prayed whether this was God's will in my life. I took counsel with my family and friends. I talked most importantly with my fiancé Irene. I knew that this was a big decision, and I did not want to make it quickly. For three weeks I wrestled with God. Every day the decision was foremost on my mind. Finally, I accepted the call and I had divine peace over the matter. I called my grandfather and said that yes, I would work for NLEC."

Chris Aaron & Irene Rice

"My first-year working has been wonderful and hard. There have been many challenges that I have had to overcome, but I learned a lot. For the first six or seven months I traveled from Springfield to St. Louis on a weekly basis. I counseled with other pastors and leaders in St. Louis. I learned a lot about leadership, fundraising, planning and spiritual growth."

"In February after completing my doctrine book and extensively being questioned by the New Life Board of Directors about my beliefs, I was ordained as a minister. Now I have the opportunity to practice what Scripture says I should do. That is one of the best parts of my job. Not every occupation allows you to face some of the trials we face when serving the poor. One example is the patience and humility necessary to serve people who are dealing with dark demons. Seeing others suffering within their spirit and stepping into that mess is not easy, but the rewards are great. Jesus himself walked the perfect life of faith, and we are associating with the same social status as Jesus."

"I am learning what it means to serve with empathy. There is very little room for pride when serving people experiencing homelessness. They can see right through the façade that works well with most other people. What I mean is this: when serving the poor, they are aware of where your heart is. You must walk with empathy to see change in those you serve. Otherwise, they have ways of humbling you. Through this job, I have learned what true empathy is. It is stepping into another's messy life and rejoicing when they rejoice and weeping when they weep. Empathy isn't easy."

"I continue to grow in my faith through this work. I know that we are doing God's work throughout Missouri. Paul says to boast in our weaknesses and to point others to Christ. This job reveals my weaknesses often, and I can boast in them to point others to Jesus. I have a long way to go in my walk of faith, but this job is the best training ground. Part of serving others is about putting their needs above your own. This is probably one of the best and hardest lessons to learn in life. Jesus came to serve, not to be served, even though he deserved to be served most. I carry this lesson with me daily."

"New Life's mission will not change. Our job is to be there when people are hurting. We will continue to meet people in their darkness and shed light to their situation. We must continue to minister to the forgotten, the lost, the broken hearted, and the homeless. In the next 50 years, I hope we can expand throughout the US. New Life can lead the way into new life in Christ. My goal is to continue to grow in faith and wisdom as we look toward the future with hope."

"Irene and I got married on January 26, 2019. Irene and I became proud parents of a little baby girl in December 2019. We named her Abigail Grace; she brings so much joy into our lives. We are still in the midst of learning how to be good parents. One of the most important lessons I have learned in my first year of work is how important a deep prayer life is. Without prayer, it is so hard to wake up and do this job. The spiritual warfare is intense in many of the locations we work at. Beyond that, this job is one of constant faith in God's provision. He has proven Himself over and over as the ultimate provider. Prayer is essential to serving the poor.

"I am honored to have the ability to serve with New Life. My family is dedicated to seeing New Life grow. It is a gift from God to serve as a pastor and leader in a ministry that makes change in the lives of thousands. As my responsibilities continue to increase, my hope is to shape better communities throughout Missouri. There is no such thing as a perfect community. I see how we need to grow and change with those around us. Yet, I am so encouraged by the legacy of change and impact New Life has had in the past. We can continue that legacy. With help from current and future partners, we can expand the work that we are doing. We must remain faithful stewards of what we have. We must also pray constantly for Christ's renewal in the broken places we serve. I have faith that the next 50 years are going to be exactly as God ordained them. I know that Christ is working in New Life, and by the power of God we will continue to grow."

What a joy it was to see how the Holy Spirit was working in Chris Aaron's life. At the same time that miracle was taking place I had to say goodbye on Saturday, March 2 at 7:40 am to my dear mother Annie Rice. She was 91 years old that day, when she looked up to heaven and then went into the eternal presence of God. It was hard to say goodbye to this precious saint, who along with my father, Lawrence had introduced me as a child to the reality of the Resurrected Christ. It wasn't until a year later, as the deadly coronavirus swept through the world that I saw how God in His faithfulness took her then to be with Him. With mother's pre-existing conditions, she would have had to suffer through the corona virus pandemic with all the restrictions it brought those who lived in assisted living facilities, such as mother did.

On Thursday, March 14 the St. Louis Board of Building Appeals voted to support the developers to stop New Life Evangelistic Center from making the repairs to re-enter 1411 Locust. This took place after NLEC had paid $3,500 to the city of St. Louis for a building permit. That money was never refunded.

Despite the Missouri Supreme Court rejecting all New Life's appeals, the financial needs, and the continual shut down of 1411 Locust, we knew God was faithful. The NLEC staff found daily strength in the promises of scripture such as that found in Isaiah 40:31 where it says, "Those who wait on the Lord shall renew their strength. They shall mount up with wings like eagles. They shall run and not be weary. They shall walk and not faint.

June 20, 2019, New Life Evangelistic Center filed an extensive application to use the former Missouri National Guard Armory at 4350 South Kingshighway, in St. Louis to help the homeless. This application was in accordance with the Steward B. McKinney Homeless Assistance Act. This law required that federal surplus property was

106

to be used for programs assisting the homeless.

Scott Egan, who later passed away in July of 2020, prepared a very extensive application. In that application, extensive research was given to document the needs of the homeless and how New Life Evangelistic Center would use this building to meet those needs. Endorsement letters of support were also included from a wide range of community leaders.

I was shocked when the application was quickly rejected by the Department of Health and Human Services. Later I learned that the City of St. Louis and the local HHS representatives had already negotiated a deal with a developer to put apartments for the upper income at that site. It never ceased to amaze me how the rich can continue to circumvent the law when it comes to robbing the homeless of something as basic as federal surplus property.

The Steward B. McKinney Homeless Assistance Act was a federal law passed during the Reagan administration to provide federal surplus property to the homeless. At this time, this law had become a political sham with less than 1% of the federal surplus property actually being used to help the homeless. It was clear the city of St. Louis had been working behind the scenes for the dismissal of NLEC's application. They did this so it would be sold to John Clancy. He had a Florida based Planet Fitness franchise. Clancy spent four million six hundred and fifty thousand dollars buying the armory and other property in the area. As the needs of the homeless were shoved aside and the federal law ignored this developer would build 2-bedroom apartments that would rent for $1,600 a month. Once again, the homeless would be robbed as the rich got richer at their expense.

It was my faith in God and His love for the poor and homeless that gave me the strength to keep going day after day, despite the obstacles. I knew from the reading of the scriptures and the study of history that ultimately justice would prevail. Even though I knew this, it was still difficult for us to hear the stories of hurting individuals like Sherleen day after day.

Sherleen in desperation pointed out to me the bug bites she had received the previous night as she slept in the park. Sherleen was homeless and since she is unable to walk, she went everywhere in her electric wheelchair. I had met her a few weeks earlier when she was immobilized since the batteries in her chair needed to be recharged, and she had nowhere she could charge them at. This time the cry for help was a cry of desperation from a woman who could no longer continue to live on the streets.

New Life was able to get Sherleen off the streets and into a place of her own as a result of those who were partnering with New Life Evangelistic Center. If it had not been for the prayers and financial support of these caring individuals, NLEC would not have been able to help Sherleen and many like her.

Kitty and her one-year-old son Dwight came to one of the New Life Evangelistic Center safe houses for women and children. After staying with NLEC for two months, Kitty and Dwight, with New Life's help were moved into their own home.

Many of these hurting and homeless people are elderly like 72-year-old Janet. When Janet shared how her children stole every cent she had and left her homeless, she would burst into tears. The only help Janet could find was at the NLEC Safe Houses for women and children.

There have been so many testimonies of how the New Life team by following Jesus into the suffering of the homeless have helped individuals in their time of need. In August I received the following from Cheryl Barban, "Happy to help your mission to assist the homeless, and people who need help, as I did in the 80's. I was working and had a one-year-old son, but I needed help. The place I was living at that time had 2 rooms with a gas stove. It was a very cold winter. I came to your center downtown St. Louis for whatever help I could receive. I was surprised that I didn't need to bring tons of paperwork to get help. In addition, everyone treated me as a human being, no shame! I got a heater to stay warm and blankets and food. Thank you and God Bless!"

On September 19 God in His faithfulness moved on Alderman Joe Vaccaro, who was chairman of the Public Safety Committee, to hold a hearing on the needs of the homeless. Ray Redlich, myself, the homeless living outside, along with other homeless advocates were able to share with this Aldermanic committee the crisis the homeless were facing daily.

On the morning of September 27, the homeless met in front of St. Louis City Hall and distributed 1,400 fliers calling for the reopening of 1411 Locust. In the afternoon Ray, Mark and myself met with Mayor Krewson and her chief of staff Steve Conway. At the meeting we explained the need to reopen 1411 Locust. Ray Redlich wrote the following report of what took place at that meeting.

"The meeting was civil. It was, indeed, the first of its kind. Topics discussed included the Biddle House, winter shelters and the Continuum of Care, as well as New Life's efforts to renovate our downtown building and re-open as a day center. Rev. Rice referred to the successful model of New Life's current center in Springfield, Missouri and the Haven of Hope in San Antonio, Texas. He even offered the possibility that New Life might be willing to sell its building on Locust Street, if a plan could be brokered that NLEC would receive five million dollars for the building and an acre plot of land from the city on which to rebuild. This proposal did not go very far, with the mayor commenting that that's a lot of money, and the city does not own that much contiguous, unused property. Rev. Rice responded that the city's Land Reutilization Authority has much more land than that."

"Ms. Krewson and Mr. Conway did refer to the city's plans to improve its winter services to the homeless, including a more consistent provision of shelter with a possibly higher temperature threshold. When Rev. Rice suggested using the Biddle House again as a day center for both men and women, they did not make any commitment or come up with an alternative."

"Overall, I saw the meeting as simply more of the same. The mayor and her administration cited what the city is currently doing for the homeless and how they plan to improve in a few areas. They really failed to acknowledge the significant part that NLEC has played over the years and could continue to play in the future. Their only specific offer was for us to participate in the Continuum of Care (which we said we would do)."

"At the end of the meeting Mayor Krewson told us that she does not want to mislead us. She really cannot foresee 1411 Locust opening. Nor, I might add, did she propose any other location from which we could operate. This is why I stated that the meeting was, 'more of the same.'"

Despite the trials and tribulations, I knew that God would continue to be faithful and true to His word. Over and over the Holy Spirit would confirm this fact as I read the scriptures, went on daily prayer walks, and in dreams I would have at night.

On November 11th I wrote the following in my journal sharing how God once again demonstrated His faithfulness. "How I praise God. Last Friday, November 8, we experienced a great miracle. Our deposits totaled $173,965. $164,221 estate came in from Nadine E. Meyer's Estate in Boonville, MO. What an answer to prayer! All the overdue bills can be paid, and salaries and stipends can be met. Oh, what a miracle working God we serve."

It was December 7, 2019, that I wrote the following in my journal. "I frequently feel so overwhelmed by all the broken lives. There is Kathy, Kolleen, Stephanie, Nancy, Zentra and her 5 children, Belinda and Brandon, the list goes on and on. Each have their own individual stories. When I feel I just can't follow Jesus with them into the midst of their pain, God reminds me I have been entrusted with them and He will never give me more than I can bear. As a result, I must daily immerse myself in the scriptures and pray.

Kathy works so hard, yet she is so fragile. She continues to be in in and out of the hospital. Kolleen came with a mountain of baggage both physical and mental. When she is pushed too hard, to clean it up she ends up back in the mental hospital. Stephanie saw her fiancée murdered and then die in her arms. Nancy needs a liver transplant and has a multitude of other physical needs.

Even with the miracle of the Nadine Meyer Estate the needs among the poor and homeless continued to mount. For that reason, it was such a privilege to see how God in His faithfulness would provide for the needs of His children through caring individuals like Donita Maxwell. Donita had resided at New Life Evangelistic Center in the late 1970's at the Park Avenue location. She was a small child and stayed there with her mother and her eight siblings! Donita remembers as a child that it was "fun" and yet, they were grateful to have food to eat and a warm place to sleep.

In the late 1980's Donita and her sister, along with their children, stayed at the New Life Evangelistic Center shelter in East St. Louis

Donita

until her family could come and help them. She spoke of remembering how cold it was that winter, and how grateful she was, once again, that she had a place of refuge to go to with her children.

Through the years, Donita has continued to be grateful for the help that New Life Evangelistic Center provided to hurting homeless women, children and men. When Donita received the life insurance money after her husband passed away, she knew she wanted ed to give back. When she walked in with her check for $15,000 for NLEC she didn't know that she was God's answer that day to the prayers of the New Life Staff.

As Donita shared her gift she said, "We must put our money where it is helping people. There are so many people in need – it could be you – we can show Jesus' love by giving. Pastor Larry Rice has been giving and helping others for many years now, God will bless you for giving to help his ministry. He (Larry Rice) is helping people both physically and helping them to know Jesus!"

My passion for the past forty-eight years was to share the gospel of Jesus Christ in word and deed with everyone I met. When the 1411 Locust building had been closed in April 2017, and KNLC sold in December of that year, I knew I had to continue sharing the good news of Christ's resurrection in every possible way. This continued to be done through 24.2, numerous social media sites, the Here's Help Radio Network and the continual printing and distribution of my weekly messages. These were also shared at www.larryriceministries.org.

On Sunday mornings Mark Glenn and I would travel throughout the downtown area distributing bags of food and the word of God. As this took place the Holy Spirit would work in the lives of the homeless and hungry we would meet.

With this desire to share the message of Christ's love with anyone and everyone I felt particularly blessed, when Kevin Killeen from KMOX radio, asked me to be a part of his 2019 KMOX Holiday Radio Show. For years Kevin had written the script for this annual production that was presented to a live audience. I was going to play myself in the production. In it I would lead a group on a winter patrol. One of the lines Kevin had written into the script was one where I would declare, "Christ was rich and became poor for our sakes and died for our sins and rose again." It was such a thrill to proclaim that reality during that holiday show.

On December 25, Christmas Day, God blessed in a mighty way as temperatures soared to 70 degrees. New Life Evangelistic Center had blocked Locust from 14th to 15th street in order that we could celebrate Christmas in front of 1411 Locust. This had also been done at Thanksgiving. Over 100 volunteers worked to help 300 homeless people. Twelve tables were set up under tents that were filled with toys and warm winter clothing. Backpacks, bus tickets, Bibles and a catered meal were also provided. At this special celebration of the birth of Christ we were able to share the good news of God's faithfulness, demonstrated through the death and resurrection of Jesus Christ.

As 2019 came to an end, all of us at New Life Evangelistic Center had once again experienced God's faithfulness in the midst of every trial and tribulation. Little did we realize as we moved into 2020 what it would mean to follow Jesus into the pain and suffering of Covid-19.

Chapter 10
Working to be there when People are Hurting

As New Life Evangelistic Center moved into a new decade, and the new year of 2020, I found myself praying more and more for the Holy Spirit to guide the New Life team as we continued to follow Jesus into the suffering and loneliness of the hurting and homeless.

Karen

Karen was one of those individuals who needed help in the most desperate way. She described how God in His grace rescued her through NLEC. "When I was rescued by New Life Evangelistic Center, I was hungry and living in a vacant house. I was cold and sick. Then God answered my prayers. Now I have a loving home with a caring family. I could have died, but now I get to help other homeless people while growing in my relationship with God. It isn't easy, I never expected to be where I am right now. I owned and ran a successful cleaning business for over 25 years when I became ill and ended up spending months at a time in the hospital with a weakened heart that only worked at 8%. My business was stolen from me while I was incapacitated and by the time I got out of the hospital, I had lost my home, my business, and my vehicles. What I have found through NLEC is Jesus, hope, and a future! I thank God for NLEC."

Not only was our Risen Lord working through New Life Evangelistic Center in the greater St. Louis area, but also in Springfield, Missouri. Terry shared the miracle God had done in her life and in the life of her son Corey. "I was homeless in Springfield, MO where my son Corey and I slept in my car. I would drive him to school each day then return in the afternoon to pick him up. After picking him up, I would find a spot to park each night where we could sleep. I tried every day, but never could get us into the family shelter. It was always full. Finally, I took my son to a children's shelter for homeless kids, and I stayed at a women's shelter."

"During that time my car was stolen. After two months in the children's shelter, the State of Missouri contacted me and said it appeared I had abandoned my child and they then threatened to take custody of him. This really hurt me because I was doing everything I could to create a home for myself and my son."

Terry & Corey

"During the day, I would go to job interviews, doctor's appointments, or go to visit my son at the children's shelter. Then I met Reverend Larry Rice and his son Chris Rice at the Veterans Coming Home Center. Later, I found out that the Veterans Coming Home Center is a division of New Life Evangelistic Center in St. Louis. I talked with Reverend Rice and his son about the leadership training program and decided it was a perfect place for myself and my son, Corey."

"Now Corey and I have stability, a home, a vehicle, and are surrounded by a loving Christian community. When I first came to NLEC, I worked with Dulce in the Development Department and then began assisting with our Social Media Department. Now I currently work as the Accounts Receivable Clerk and assist Charlie Hale. I manage one of the Safe Houses for women and children, and I provide transportation for some of the ladies staying at the safe houses."

"God allowed the bad things I went through to provide a testimony of how He works for good in our lives. Now I love sharing my how Jesus provided for me when I was homeless. This shows how Christ works through the lives of caring people like the partners and staff at New Life Evangelistic Center."

Miguel was one of the growing numbers of homeless individuals that the team of NLEC first responders were helping on a daily basis. Miguel was in the army and stationed in Iraq. While he was on active duty there he ran over a live mine and saw his friend instantly killed. After this, Miguel would have nightmares and now was homeless with mental problems.

Neil described how by being in the NLEC residential living program he was drawing closer to God, "I came to New Life a broken man. Alcoholism had destroyed my relationships and caused me to lose my job. Since I have been at New Life, I have found healing and recovery from alcoholism and from my anger. Now, I live in peace. To God be the glory for the great things He has done in my life!"

It was bitter cold outside when on January 31, 2020 the doors were opened at City Hall to the homeless. The homeless were then able to come in out of the freezing weather to participate in the NLEC Life Skills Class for the homeless. Alderman Joe Vaccarro made it possible for New Life to use Room 202 to help the homeless. As the life skills class took place for the ninety homeless people present, two aldermen visited the meeting and saw how the transportation needs of the homeless were being met by New Life Evangelistic Center.

While I was preparing to engage in church on the streets with Mark Glenn Sunday, February 2, I received a text from Ray at 7 am. In it he told me about Quinton Carter, who had been struck by a car Friday night. Quinton was, hit as he was, trying to save a woman who had been struck by a hit and run driver at 13th and Cass. The woman died instantly while Quinton was taken to the hospital severely injured. After Quinton was released from the hospital Ray had tried to get Quinton into a shelter, but none were available.

Quinton

Ray had asked me to look for Quinton at a homeless encampment beside the old Greyhound bus station on Tucker and Cass. When Mark and I arrived there, we found that at least three homeless individuals were living there. When I called Quinton's name he moved and pulled back his blankets and told me he had come here from Louisiana to attend his father's funeral. While here his car had been stolen and he ended up homeless. Now Quinton was trying to survive outside with head, jaw, and leg injuries. After leaving Quinton with food, money, warm clothing, and other supplies I knew we had to get him back to his home in Louisiana.

Ray and I continued to assist Quinton throughout the week. Then on the following Friday he was honored by the Board of Aldermen for trying to save Emily Coffee. I also spoke to the Board about why 1411 Locust needed to reopen immediately. In addition, I stressed how we had to get shelter for Quinton and many others who were suffering homelessness in the city of St. Louis. After Quinton concluded his surgeries the following week, New Life Evangelistic Center helped him return to his family in Louisiana.

As the needs among the homeless continued to grow so did the financial needs of the New Life Evangelistic Center. A multitude of bills including 12 that were shut off notices for utilities at NLEC Safe Houses existed. New Life was also a week behind in paying the salaries of employees. These needs were taken by the NLEC Staff and myself to our Heavenly Father in earnest prayer as we stood on the promise of Philippians 4:19. "My God shall supply all your needs according to His glorious riches in Christ Jesus." After praying for over an hour Wednesday, February 13 and asking God to forgive every known and unknown sin I had committed, we saw the first of a series of financial miracles. New Life Evangelistic Center received $12,000 in donations. This was a tremendous blessing, but the pile of bills continued to grow larger. I knew I had to remain faithful and encourage the NLEC Staff to do the same as the Holy Spirit showed us that we had to trust Jesus in every area of our lives.

The next day, $4,500 came in. Friday, when it was 8 degrees outside, God provided an additional $9,000. As the Lord continued to provide financially, it became increasingly clear as time passed that the Board of Alderman had no intention of helping New Life get back into 1411 Locust. The downtown business interests were doing everything they could to stop all efforts to reopen this building to the homeless. They preferred to have these individuals wander the streets of downtown rather than have them get the help they needed at New Life Evangelistic Center.

The war against the hurting and homeless was not only in the city of St. Louis, but in St. Louis County. It was for that reason that Mark, Karen, Janet and myself went to the St. Louis County Council meeting on Tuesday, February 18 to try to get the county to remove its vagrancy laws. Even though we testified why those laws needed to be revoked, no action was taken by the County Council.

As the New Life Evangelistic Center staff worked to meet the growing needs throughout Mid-America, an epidemic was spreading throughout China that would directly impact the life of every citizen in the United States. On March 15, 2020, I wrote the following in my journal.

"Life is being turned upside down in America as a result of the corona virus or COVID-19. From Broadway to baseball, events are being cancelled. I was discovering even churches are being closed. Today when I visited a large church in Maryland Heights, Missouri I was surprised to see the parking lot empty. When I went inside a video of a previous service was being shown but no one was there to see it."

Life as we knew it in America was being turned upside down. No one knew of a cure for this deadly disease that was killing thousands of people around the world. Mask mandates were going into effect. As lock downs were taking place, we were determined that the New Life Evangelistic Center would continue helping the hurting and homeless.

Ray Redlich wrote the following concerning NLEC's outreach during the pandemic, "New Life Evangelistic Center has always strived to 'be there when people are hurting.' The COVID-19 pandemic is no exception."

"In my ministry of homeless street outreach. I go out several times a week with my partners Chris Ohnimus and David Williams. We witness the challenges that the homeless face that seem insurmountable even when conditions are 'normal'. How much more so when society as a whole is 'shut down.'"

"At a time when everyone was being told to stay at home, the homeless might be easily forgotten. But New Life Evangelistic Center continued its vital outreach, recognizing that this outreach is an essential function during the pandemic."

"Of course, our workers took precautions, donning face masks and remembering to keep a safe distance as much as possible. But we also gave out the necessary tools to safeguard the health our homeless friends – hand sanitizer, masks (lovingly made in volunteers' homes), food and water. Our purpose was always to let the homeless know that they were not forgotten."

"In some instances, I heard homeless persons express a fatalistic attitude, as if to say, 'COVID 19 is the least of my problems; I'll die from something else first.' In such cases it is important for us to affirm their worth, reminding them that God truly cares about them."

"That is why our daily presence in their midst, myself, and my co-workers, along with Reverend Larry Rice and other staff, means so much. Just by being there, praying with them, sharing material water as well as the Living Water, we are able to demonstrate hope and the reality of Christ's love."

"Yes, this is an unprecedented time. But as we continue to seek out creative ways to meet human needs, we can serve as a bridge to those who are hurting."

It was March 18 that Ray and I had a press conference in front of the St. Louis city hall. At the press conference we announced we were distributing 2,500 hygiene kits to the homeless throughout Mid-America. These kits included hand sanitizer which the New Life Staff were making from rubbing alcohol and aloe vera gel. This was necessary because it was almost impossible to buy hand sanitizer in the stores. The kits also included wash clothes, soap, bottled water and other hygiene items. Bags of food would be given out with shelter at the NLEC safe houses provided. Four St. Louis television stations attended the press conference along with KMOX radio.

In Springfield my son Chris, and my grandson Chris Aaron, were told as they directed the NLEC work there, that they would only be allowed to have ten individuals in 806 North Jefferson at a time. As a result of this mandate by the City of Springfield they moved the New Life Evangelistic Center services outside. They then rotated in ten individuals at a time to use the showers and other services provided inside. Meals and other assistance were provided for the homeless in the parking lot.

In the midst of this crisis, I found strength in passages like Isaiah 41:10 which says, "Fear not, for I am with you. Be not dismayed for I am your God. I will strengthen you. Yes, I will uphold you with my righteous, right hand."

I shared the following with the community and the staff of New Life Evangelistic Center as COVID-19 continued to spread. "As we live in a worldwide pandemic of coronavirus, we must not forget that God has made it possible for us to go through life planting seeds of hope. That is what we are striving to do at New Life Evangelistic Center through the gifts and prayers of caring people like you."

"At New Life Evangelistic Center, we are working to plant these seeds of hope. This is being done through the provision of food, shelter, job training programs etc. as we share the hope provided through Scriptures. The scriptures include Psalms 31:24 where it says, "Be strong, and take heart, all you who hope in the Lord.""

"Planting seeds of hope involves reflecting on God the creator who daily sustains each individual human being, animal, and flower. This meditation enables us to grasp the words of Jesus when He says in Matthew 6:30, 31, "If that is how God clothes the grass of the field which is here today and tomorrow is thrown into the fire, will He not much more clothe you, O you of little faith.""

Chris Aaron described the work of New Life Evangelistic Center in Springfield, Missouri during COVID-19. "The pandemic seemed so distant and foreign at first. There was very little substantial and fact-based information about the strange new virus in Wuhan, China. The virus didn't impact our work in Springfield throughout February, when talk was silent about this deadly sickness. When Italy got hit hard by COVID-19 there were ominous warnings wringing in the news. Before then, not much news even covered the virus. Our government seemed blatantly unconcerned about it, so why should we worry? In March the news really began to consume our lives." "Then March 15th hit and the whole world seemed to be in panic. There was no gradual shift from ambivalence to fear. Instead, it became nearly impossible to buy toilet paper and hand sanitizer overnight. When the city of Springfield dropped the number of people that could gather from 50 to 10 in two days, it changed the way we could operate entirely. On March 19th, rain poured down in sheets as the New Life Evangelistic Center staff and I set up big tent pavilions to serve the homeless outside. Some of those we served pitched in to help in the drenching, cold rain. When we got the tents set up, we served breakfast to around 80 individuals. The two pavilions helped provide a slight respite from the downpour. Throughout the closure of Springfield, the NLEC Veterans Coming Home Center remained open to 7 individuals in the building. They could use a bathroom, call a friend, check their mail, and get some dry clothes. We also served breakfast every day outside. Many volunteers and partnering agencies helped us serve those most in need."

"As a city, Springfield responded as quickly as possible to the coronavirus. I was in daily communication with other nonprofits fighting to keep the homeless safe through this difficult time. For the first three weeks there was no place for the homeless to take a shower. Through our help, we were able to provide showers at a pool close to our building. The NLEC Veterans Coming Home Center continued to be a help during this hard, painful time. There seemed to be very little direction from the Federal government and lots of confusion as to what we should do. The local government did their best, but it seemed the homeless were less on their mind than the businesses now closed. In a hopeless situation, the New Life Evangelistic Center strived to meet the basic needs of individuals. We went to homeless camps, bringing essential items that bring life and hope. We drove around Springfield, searching for individuals who walked until they could go no further to give them sustenance and help."

To get a better understanding of how the COVID-19 pandemic was impacting Mid-America and NLEC response to it let me share with you the following entries from my journal.

Tuesday, April 7, "The coronavirus has killed at least 12,893 people in the United States. 1,736 died just today in the USA. The USA has more cases than any other country, with over 398,000 people who are diagnosed with COVID-19. Worldwide more than 1.42 million people have been diagnosed with COVID-19 and at least 82,074 have died since the virus emerged in China in December. The actual numbers are believed to be even higher due to testing shortages. Italy has the world's highest death toll – over 17,100. The UK Prime Minister Boris Johnson is hospitalized by COVID-19. San Diego has turned the San Diego Convention Center into a shelter for the homeless."

"A tent community has risen in St. Louis between Tucker and 15th Street on Market Street. Mayor Krewson is criticizing the tents, but such is essential. NLEC first responders are trying to help the homeless with sandwiches, water, hygiene kits."

Thursday, April 9, "Today in the USA twin epidemics are taking place. There have been 16.8 million jobs lost in the last 3 weeks. The economy is in free fall. There have been 6.6 million unemployment claims. Over 16,200 deaths have taken place. 424,000 cases of COVID-19 have now been reported. They expect the COVID cases will peak by this Easter Sunday. The day we celebrate the resurrection is supposed to be the day with the peak of deaths. Yet through Christ there is hope. His death and His resurrection is the hope we have both now and for all eternity."

"Tomorrow, Good Friday, we once again rally in front of city hall with the homeless. We will be sharing the love of Christ, with masks and gloves on and social distancing in place. I want t o share with all that there is hope because Christ is Risen. There were 3,737 cases and 88 deaths in Missouri and 534 deaths today in Illinois."

Friday, April 10, "This has been a Good Friday unlike any other Good Friday. No church services. Record numbers of people who are un-employed. Today the staff and I gathered outside city hall with masks and gloves on – I did a Good Friday show that featured the home-less and the tent community which the police tried to shut down at 4 am yesterday morning. Resistance by the homeless, volunteers and a lawyer caused the police to back down. The politicians knew that shutting down the tent community would be a direct violation of CDC guidelines."

"Ray helped place a family of five at the Roadway Inn for a week. Handicapped members of the family had been living with their moth-er in their van in the middle of the corona virus crisis. Then the motel cancelled the deal because of the children. This is a time when we must trust God and reach out to those in need through His love. Over 100,000 worldwide have died. There have been 18,637 US deaths, 98 deaths in Missouri and 601 deaths in Illinois."

Monday, April 13, "Yesterday, Easter was unlike any other Easter. I spent the morning with Mark, David, and James visiting encamp-ments of homeless throughout downtown St. Louis giving out back packs filled with hygiene items, food, flashlights, etc. The first family I met across from city hall in the park at Chestnut and Tucker was a mother with her three children. They were living in a van with two bro-ken out windows. After visiting camps along Market Street, we went to four other locations where homeless people were living. As I was reflecting on Easter with Debra I thought of the similarities between the coronavirus and the crucifixion. Both dying from "respiratory" breathing issues. Jesus died after his legs were broken after he hung on the cross and could no longer push up to take a breath of air. Both Christ's deaths and those dying from COVID 19 are dying very lonely deaths."

Friday, April 17, "22,000,000 Americans are now unemployed. How many more will end up without jobs? Today I visited the river front homeless village which continues to grow and grow with so many homeless people. I praise God for how He continues to miraculously supply. Two weeks ago, upon completing a prayer walk in Lafayette Park. I encountered Robert N. He had donated in the past. He saw our encounter as a divine appointment. This past week he sent $10,000. Praise the Lord for His goodness!"

"The USA now has over 716,000 cases with over 38,000 deaths. 5,562 cases in Missouri with over 190 deaths due to the coronavirus. In Illinois it has been over 29,600 cases and over 1,259 deaths. NLEC continues to help the homeless during COVID-19. God is a miracle working God. Since February I have been waiting on the Almighty to perform a $200,000 miracle. I placed that need at Philippians 4:19 that 'My God shall provide all our needs according to His riches and glory in Christ Jesus.' In April He provided $44,217 from the estate of Kenneth and Joy Ferguson. Today, Charlie Hale, our financial administrator, got word that next Monday NLEC is to receive a check for $121,991 as part of the government stimulus money to help small businesses like NLEC to cover its next six payrolls. Ten days from now NLEC is to close on the radio station being sold in Van Buren for $40,000. This totals $206,208. Praise the Lord! Thank you, Jesus!"

Monday, April 27 "Today I was in Springfield with Chris Aaron working with the homeless feeding them breakfast at the NLEC Center. Then we went to the homeless camps in the woods in Springfield. So many people are living in tents. Yesterday I went with Mark, James and David in St. Louis to homeless camps and vacant buildings. Met two men, one living in a tent and another in a vacant building who want to go to where the NLEC men's program is in New Bloomfield. Ray met one today who went to New Bloomfield with another coming Wednesday. Three came since last Thursday. Two from Springfield and one from Teen Challenge. Today I talked to my sister Carolyn, she said that 140 cases of COVID-19 had struck the nursing home where mother had been plus the nursing home next to that one. The 140 includes residents, staff and family members who had visited them. If mother had not passed away March 2, 2019, she would be so miserable now."

Despite warnings by the Center for Disease Control (CDC) not to destroy homeless encampments during the COVID-19 pandemic St. Louis Mayor Krewson announced that her administration was going to take steps to do such. The tent communities she directed her declaration of destruction at were those on Market Street.

For nearly a month the homeless had lived in tents across from the mayor's office at Market and Tucker. Another homeless encampment had developed at 14th and Market Street. Both camps had illustrated how the homeless could live and work together in community. It had given those who lived in these communities a sense of belonging and some control over their lives. With a tent they could keep their belongings in and the freedom the homeless had to come and go as they please they felt their dignity and self-worth return.

At 10:15 am Friday, May 1 Mayor Lydia Krewson's top aids Steve Conway and Todd Waltermann attacked the homeless community at 14th and Market with backup from the police department. Their intentions were to shut down this homeless encampment with promises they would give those living there a place to go. To their surprise the people living there had gotten a taste of self-respect and refused to go. The situation became particularly intense when Todd Waltermann got in the face of two of the homeless women and with the arrogance of a rich powerful man made his demands. The women responded to his arrogance and domineering attitude and in a matter of moments the interaction escalated. Seeing they were on the verge of a riot, Steve Conway pulled Waltermann to the side along with the commanding officer. The result was the police and the mayor's representatives left. The Arch City Defenders then filed a restraining order in federal court.

The next day the federal judge, believing the city's claim it was providing for the homeless, did not grant the restraining order. Hearing this, the homeless proceeded to take down their tents and scatter throughout the downtown area. A few went to the Best Western hotel which the city operated with a police presence. Others sought refuge along the river front and in vacant buildings.

One of the riverfront homeless encampments was started by a

woman in her forties who just wanted a home of her own. The city refused to allow a dumpster to be placed near that homeless community, as a result, the trash piled up and the rats multiplied.

On Sunday, May 10 David, James, and I filled the NLEC pick up with food, hygiene items, and even flat fixit for the bikes that the homeless on the river front. Morgan St. Peters, the woman who had created this river front community had requested these items. Ray and Judy Redlich met us at the river front encampment and joined us for a worship service among the homeless living there. It was wonderful to see the Holy Spirit move among God's homeless people.

Even though COVID-19 was continuing its death and destruction the faithfulness of God was at work at New Life Evangelistic Center. Increasing numbers of homeless people were getting involved in the NLEC residential training program. Lapsed donors were returning and donations were going up as individuals saw the New Life team members on the front lines helping the homeless and hurting during COVID-19.

On May 25, George Floyd, a 46-year-old black man was killed by Minneapolis police officers as he was unarmed and handcuffed. He cried out three times he could not breath as three policemen held him down with one having his knee on Floyd's neck.

In the days following, Black Lives Matter protests took place all over the United States. In Mid-America the NLEC staff continued to plant seeds of hope and reconciliation during COVID-19. Twenty three percent of the victims of the corona virus were African Americans. At the same time, 44% of the African America community were declaring they had lost their job or were suffering economically. As one thirty-one-year-old African declared, "It's either COVID 19 killing us, cops are killing us, or the economy is killing us."

Because of those who were faithfully sharing with New Life Evangelistic Center our first responder volunteers and staff were able to daily meet the needs of the hurting and homeless. This not only included those coming to 806 N. Jefferson in Springfield but also the homeless sleeping outside in the greater St. Louis area. As these direct services were being provided God made it possible for NLEC to release a 69-page booklet entitled, "Planting Seeds of Hope and Love During COVID-19." It consisted of inspirational messages and a multitude of testimonies from the previously homeless. These lives had been changed through the love of Christ working in the NLEC residential training program.

June 30, at approximately 4 am Richard Dean, a 48-year-old homeless man who used a walker was crossing East Chestnut near the NLEC center in Springfield. As Richard crossed the street, he was hit and killed by a hit and run driver. Scarlet Turner, who was with Richard, ran out to help him when he was hit. As Scarlet ran out to help Richard she was struck down by another car and died. Both homeless individuals would come daily to the New Life Evangelistic Center Veterans Coming Home Center. A memorial service was held for them a few days later at this center at 806 N. Jefferson.

Saturday morning, July 13 at 6:10 am Scott Egan a veteran on our NLEC team, died of cancer due to the agent orange he received while in the military in Vietnam. Scott was a faithful member of the NLEC staff who helped in so many ways. He was truly a gift from God that had been sent to serve at New Life Evangelistic Center.

One of the only ministers to be with us when the city of St. Louis closed the New Life Evangelistic Center shelter at 1411 Locust was Cori Bush. On August 4 Cori beat the 52-year-old Clay congressional dynasty to win the Democratic primary for Congress. She later went on to win the election in November and became a United States Congresswoman.

Due to the corona virus, public water fountains had been shut off and indoor dining, where the homeless could get water was becoming almost impossible to find. One homeless man I met on a hot August day was no desperate for water he had been chewing on a piece of gum he had found on the ground. I gave this man several bottles of water. It was then I became even more determined to see that every person who remained outside homeless received the water they needed.

One lady I gave water to a few days later drank the whole bottle in front of me in less than a minute. She told me she had not had a drink of water for 30 hours. Those who were homeless with no money to buy water were often left thirsty unless the New Life first responders took water to them.

When the homeless and hurting don't get enough water, their body experiences a breakdown that can span from headache, dry skin and dizziness to a rapid heart rate, lethargy, confusion, seizures, and shock.

Because of those who gave to New Life Evangelistic Center, over 500 homeless people in Mid-America were given cold water each day. One of these individuals was Haley, who was overjoyed when she received water in her time of need. Jesus promised in Matthew 10:42, "Whoever gives one of these little ones even a cup of cold water will by no means lose their reward."

Tammy, was another one of God's homeless children, who was very thankful for the cold water she received during COVID-19.

Eugene, who lost his fingers and toes to frost bite, praised God for the water he received. He was sitting on a hot sidewalk in front of the homeless Jesus statue when he was found by the New Life first responders.

Tammy

Locked out of the 1411 Locust building by the developers, condo owners, and politicians, the homeless were not only struggling to get a place to sleep but even a drink of water. On Sunday, August 23, the St. Louis Post-Dispatch featured the violence in downtown in an article entitled, "The Wild Wild West". It shared how the city had to block off from the 12th to the 14th block of Washington using concrete barricades to try to stop the drag racing and shootings. I began to ask myself if this violence was part of God's judgement on downtown St. Louis for the way it treated the homeless?

Downtown big money interests had blamed the homeless for the petty crimes in 2016 and the first part of 2017. They had made a case that things would improve by closing the last major walk-in shelter and refuge for the homeless at 1411 Locust. When they accomplished this goal things only gotten worse. Those who believed that God is a just God recognized how His judgement had now fallen on those special interests who have allowed their greed to drive the poor and homeless out of their shelter. The Scriptures made it clear, God was not pleased with how His homeless children were being treated.

What a blessing it was to see the people of God now partnering with New Life Evangelistic Center to help buy water, hygiene items, bus tickets, masks, and other essential supplies for the homeless. As the COVID 19 pandemic swept through Mid America, New Life Evangelistic Center was also trying to help those in India who were suffering.

The director of New Life Evangelistic Center in India, Paparao Yelruchi shared how NLEC in that country was responding to the COVID-19 pandemic. He wrote, "It is a very difficult situation in India. New Life Evangelistic Center is visiting door to door and helping those in need with food bags, soap, sanitizer, and face masks as part of the COVID-19 relief work. We are interacting with the people as we are planting seeds of hope from the written word of God. The homeless, the young adults, teenagers are committing suicide due to lack of hope in their life."

"At this Corona virus time, since India is locked down completely, the rich people purchase their food materials well in advance. The poor, the homeless, the lepers, the hopeless widows, street children, they do not have any hope and they do not have money to purchase food material as the rich does. As many are suffering from hunger, New Life Evangelistic Center is providing these needy people with food bags and the word of God."

"We encourage them with scriptures like Psalm 84:11 where it says, "For the Lord God is a sun and shield, the Lord will give grace and glory, no good thing will He withhold from those who walk uprightly, I will love you, O Lord, you are my strength."

"Also, Psalm 18:2 which declares, "The Lord is my rock, my fortress and my deliverer; my God is my rock, in whom I take refuge, my shield and the horn of my salvation, my stronghold."

"We encourage the people of India to know the hope Ephesians 1:18 speaks of when it says, "I pray that the eyes of your heart may be enlightened in order that you may know the hope to which he has called you, the riches of his glorious inheritance in his holy people."

"To give hope and love, New Life Evangelistic Center is conducting corona virus relief work by meeting the needs of the depressed, homeless and many other needy people. We are giving food bags, soap, sanitizers, to over 600 people so far. Thousands are now need your help more than ever before."

As we took these needs to God in prayer, we saw Him respond to the major financial needs of the New Life Evangelistic Center in a wide variety of ways. In the middle of September, New Life Evangelistic Center received $31,485.32 from the Ike and June Hallman Trust. In addition, the Lord made it possible for NLEC to sell a building in Columbia for $153,500. These miracles plus the prayers and faithful support of the New Life partners made it possible fore even more hurting, homeless people to be helped through the work of New Life Evangelistic Center.

As fall turned to winter New Life began several new programs to help the homeless survive during the cold winter months. This included intensifying efforts to get the homeless into their own homes by developing a Home for Christmas Program.

Cheryl and her 24-year-old daughter Rachel lost their jobs due to COVID-19 and subsequently became homeless. "I thank God for NLEC!" said Cheryl. Because of caring donors who partnered with New Life Evangelistic Center, Cheryl, her 15-year-old son, Mack, and her daughter, Rachel, were able to be in a place of their own for Christmas.

The Boyd family who received a house from NLEC said, "Our family has had its share of troubles over the past years. There was a time when we were homeless and had to live separately. After COVID-19 hit, I was laid off from my job. New Life Evangelistic Center helped us to get into a house of our own and blessed us with a gift to help towards Christmas presents for the kids."

Cheryl & Rachel

Julie explained, "I would have died if I didn't get the help I needed from the NLEC Veterans Coming Home Center in Springfield, Missouri. I suffer from PTSD and Anxiety and have escaped a terribly abusive relationship. I thank God for NLEC and the Home for Christmas Program! Now I know I will be safe surrounded by family and friends!"

The Boyd Family

New Life Evangelistic Center also helped many poor and elderly individuals stay in their own homes by helping them pay their utility bills. Jerri and Christina are just two of those who were helped.

Jerry explained, "I came to New Life seeking financial assistance for our utility bill. Due to COVID-19, our income has been reduced in our household. As a result of New Life Evangelistic Center's help, I will be able to prevent our utilities from being disconnected. Our family is grateful to God and NLEC for helping us at a time of need."

Christina said, "I came to NLEC because I've been struggling financially for the past 4 months. My child has not been able to go to his daycare because of COVID-19. This has made it hard for me to work. New Life is helping me to get caught up with my gas bill. Thank you, New Life for helping me in my time of need!"

In November New Life Evangelistic Center working with the Ozark Partnership and the city of Springfield extended its hours of service at 806 N. Jefferson. When the weather was below 30 degrees the center stayed open until 8 pm at which time buses would take the homeless to shelters and bring them back the next morning at 8 am. The prayers of the New Life Staff were that in the not-too-distant future they would see the city of St. Louis work with NLEC in the same cooperative way.

How we praised God for the miracle of a $120,000 estate that came in the middle of November. We were then able to get another safe house, expand the New Life Evangelistic

Christina with her son, Roman

Center's Home for Christmas Program and get a ventilator for the hospital New Life was operating for COVID patients in India.

Vincent was one of the stranded travelers NLEC was able to get home for Christmas. We found Vincent sleeping in front of city hall. Vincent said he was so depressed he was thinking of committing suicide. In a matter of hours, the NLEC team had Vincent on a bus back to Utah.

The year 2020 provided believers in the risen Christ unprecedented opportunities to share the love of God to the hurting and homeless.

129

As they partnered with the New Life Evangelistic Center with their prayers, financial gifts, and volunteer services, we were able to be there when people were hurting. What a joy it was to see the Spirit of God do exceedingly more than we could have ever imagined. This miracle took place as the love of God poured forth into the lives of the hurting and homeless when believers shared their faith in word and acts of compassion.

Chapter 11
God's Faithfulness Continues in the Midst of the Trials and Tribulations

Kim

While Kim was homeless, she had been raped six times. After being at a New Life Evangelistic Center Safe House and growing in her faith in Christ, Kim felt it was time for her to return to her home at the end of 2020. What a joy it was to see how the Spirit of God had not only healed Kim personally but also her relationship with her family.

When I awakened January 1, 2021, the Lord was speaking to my spirit that in the new year New Life Evangelistic Center was to move forth by faith and help even more hurting and homeless people.

That morning as I joined the NLEC staff at 6:45 am in front of the St. Louis City Hall, it was 33 degrees with ice covering all the trees. As I prayed for the Holy Spirit to lead me, I met a homeless woman whose son had been murdered just a few weeks earlier. When she showed me his picture the Spirit of God laid it on my heart that we had to give that woman the last $300 she needed to get into an apartment.

Then, someone pointed out Willie to me. Willie was sitting at the bus stop in front of city hall. As I talked to Willie, I learned she had slept in that bus stop in the freezing weather the previous night. I then invited her to one of the New Life safe houses.

As I was talking to Willie a man nearby overheard us and then proceeded to tell me how he had slept on a light blanket the night before in Forest Park. This homeless man was then taken to a motel along with the other homeless individuals.

To those who would ask, "in the long term does any of this really make any different in the lives of these homeless people," I would point to Denise Lewis. Denise is one of our friends on Facebook who regularly responds to NLEC's Facebook live videos. She wrote, "I became homeless when my family kicked me out due to my rebellion.

One of my mom's neighbors brought me to the New Life Evangelistic Center on Park Avenue in 1983. It was there that I met Rev. Larry Rice and his family. They had shared the gospel with me and told me about the Training Program. I decided I wanted to join, and I went to the Women's Farm. There I helped take care of sheep and two goats named Abby and Rita. It was at the NLEC Farm that I learned how to milk a goat! That is also where I gave my life to the Lord."

"When I was brought back to the city, I went to live at 2107 Park Avenue with the Rice family. During the day I would go to 1411 Locust to help with the mailings and perform other jobs like cleaning the offices. I also babysat Larry and Penny's children, Stephanie, Jennifer and Chris. I was part of this ministry for about 5 years. While I was there, God showed me His love in a way that only Christ could. All the time I was there everyone treated me like I was part of their family. My fondest memories of living at New Life is getting to spend so much time with the Rice family. I enjoyed riding bikes with Chris when he was 12 years old. I also discovered what God's plan was for me while I was part of New Life."

Denise is just one of the many who the Holy Spirit had brought into the work of New Life Evangelistic Center during its first 49 years. In 2021 New Life Evangelistic Center first responders continued ministering to many homeless individuals on a daily basis.

When Ray Redlich and I traveled to Perryville, Missouri on January 29th to get our COVID-19 vaccinations. Ray told me about Matthew, who lived in a tent in a south city cemetery. While Matthew slept in the tent, a coyote had stuck its nose in that tent at 3 am. Matthew then hit the coyote hard in the nose and it took off.

As we traveled, Ray also told me about the vacant building called Raccoonville. It was called that because of the number of raccoons which came out at night while the homeless were sleeping. Bebe, a homeless woman who lived there always made sure that any homeless person who needed help was welcome there.

Raccoonville reminded me of John who had lived for the past few years in a vacant warehouse between the railroad tracks near the Mississippi River. John had his dog, chickens and in the summer months a small garden. Earlier in the year John had been hit by a car as he was walking back to his "vaco". Recently a mentally ill man had come into John's residency and for no reason beat him until two other homeless men had chased the intruder off. Despite all his troubles John still asked for three tents so he could set them up in the vacant warehouse so other homeless people would have a place to stay.

Candice was a homeless woman that Ray, the NLEC homeless patrol team and myself would visit regularly. Candice lived in a tent under the highway 70 overpass. She was a woman in her fifties who Ray

Candice

had spent many hours working to help overcome her addiction to alcohol. Our prayers were being answered as Candice cut back her alcohol consumption and the promise of a tiny house for her was becoming a reality.

When the temperature dropped close to zero degrees between February 11 to the 15th I cried out to God for help. That a miracle took place as New Life Evangelistic Center received a check for $15,000 from Steve Goedeker. That blessing was immediately put to work. Homeless people living outside in the subfreezing temperatures were put into motels. These individuals included Angela Burnett and her three children who were living in their car. Bryan and Angela were also living in their car along with Hannah and Ryan who were trying to survive in a vacant building. There were others like the mother who had no place to go with her two-year-old son. Charles who was homeless in a wheelchair with no legs needed help and many others. What a joy it was to see the love of Christ working in the lives of the homeless as those God had blessed shared with the work of New Life Evangelistic Center.

As the miracles took place so did the trials and tribulations. Since November of 2016 the homeless Jesus statue stood in front of 1411 Locust in St. Louis. It was a bronze statue of Jesus and his nail pierced feet sleeping on a park bench. This homeless Jesus statue comforted the afflicted and afflicted the comfortable as people walked down the street or cars passed by. Those afflicted were the ones who wanted the homeless out of sight and out of mind.

Early on the morning of March 3 an attempt was made to steal the homeless Jesus statue. As this happened a neighbor on the ninth floor of the building at 15th and Locust heard a saw cutting off the four legs of the bench the statue of Jesus was on. The woman observing the thieves yelled and the thieves went a block down the street only to return. The woman then called the police who arrested the robber.

The man who confessed to this crime was later released only to return three days later with additional help. The thieves then completed sawing off the last leg of the bronze statue right above where it was anchored in the concrete sidewalk.

The homeless Jesus statue was then taken to Illinois where it was cut up to be sold for scrap. New Life did get the pieces of the statue back later, but the cost of reassembling it made such an impossibility. Although authorities knew who the thieves were, no one was apprehended or convicted of the crime of stealing and cutting up the homeless Jesus. The whole event symbolizes how Jesus who came as the homeless one is treated daily by those He gave His life for.

Despite the daily trials and tribulations, God continued to perform the miraculous. In the midst of the tremendous financial needs Donna who represented the estate of Kingsley Holman came to the Overland Center in the middle of March and informed me that Kingsley had left New Life Evangelistic Center over $200,000 which NLEC would receive later in 2021. This was just one more miracle that God would provide in order for New Life Evangelistic Center to be there when people are hurting.

On March 26, as I was in the parking lot of the NLEC Overland headquarters thanking God for His many blessings, an African American woman in an older model car arrived in the parking lot. Getting out of the car she told me her name was Dorinda Maxwell and she had something for NLEC. Then she handed me a check made payable to New Life Evangelistic Center for $15,000.

This was a great miracle in answer to the prayers to continue to pay the bills NLEC had due. Dorinda then went on to tell me that when she was a child, her mother and her were homeless and they stayed at NLEC in the 1970's. Then in the 1980's as a young adult she ended up homeless in bitter cold weather and had stayed at the New Life

Evangelistic Center in East St. Louis with her children. Dorinda said she never forgot the help she received and now after her husband died, she wanted to share from the life insurance money she received. This miracle once again showed me I did not need to worry for God had everything under control.

Since 1988 New Life Evangelistic Center had been sharing the love of Christ in India. Since that time NLEC in India had grown tremendously as it daily assisted the orphans, widows, hurting and homeless. In April 2021, the country of India was being ravished by the corona virus. The New Life Evangelistic Center India Director, Paparao Yeleshuri had teamed up with a local hospital that was being overwhelmed by COVID-19 patients. NLEC in America assisted Paparao in acquiring, with the help of Ed Baker, six urgently needed ventilators for the New Foundation Hospital.

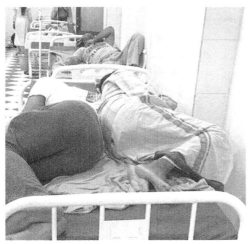

In the midst of the miracles there were also trials, tribulations and tragedies. One of these took place June 17 when Jeff and Tom were involved in a major traffic accident on highway 44 west of Rolla. They were traveling back from Marshfield when the trailer they were pulling

started weaving back and forth on the highway. When the truck went off the road down an incline and hit a tree, Jeff's air bag did not engage on the passenger's side. As a result, the dashboard was shoved back to the point both of Jeff's legs were smashed. A lady seeing the accident called 911 and an ambulance was on the scene in less than 3 minutes. Then a helicopter was called in to fly Jeff to the University hospital in Columbia. It was there he experienced his first of what would be many operations. As this took place, the NLEC team went into immediate prayer for Jeff Schneider's total recovery.

Six weeks later, Mike speaks and his family went to the hospital with COVID-19. Mike had become a mighty leader at the men's residential training center in New Bloomfield.

Mike's wife Alexius and his son Ben were released from the hospital after a few days. Mike remained at the Veterans hospital in Columbia until he was transferred to an extended housing unit in St. Louis. There he was to have received help for his extensive breathing problems. Four days after the transfer, Mike Speaks died.

When a memorial service was held in New Bloomfield, I was surprised at the number of people that had come from the community. Benjamin's Scout Master and coach were there along with many others. As the service took place it was clear that Mike's witness of the love of Christ had impacted a large number of many people for the glory of God.

The Spiritual battles continued when on September 11th, following Mike Speaks funeral and burial at Jefferson Barracks Veterans Cemetery, the barn in New Bloomfield burned down. Although the barn was a total loss, we thanked God that no one or none of the animals were injured.

Despite the trials and tribulations, I marveled at how God continued to provide each and every day. One of these miracles in the month of September involved Robert, who I encountered while on a prayer walk on the northern side of Tower Grove Park. I was taking a major financial need I had on my heart to the Lord in prayer when Robert passed by me riding his bicycle. Recognizing me he pulled over and we began to talk. As he pulled away, he declared he was going to bring a check to the New Life Evangelistic Center headquarters for $10,000. I then proceeded to praise God for His faithfulness.

Five days later, Robert came to the Center and dropped off his check. It wasn't for $10,000 but $20,000. What a miracle working God we serve!

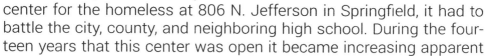

As the New Life Evangelistic Center staff moved by faith into October, we continued to see God's miraculous provision take place not only in the greater St. Louis area but also in Springfield, Missouri.

When New Life Evangelistic Center opened the day center for the homeless at 806 N. Jefferson in Springfield, it had to battle the city, county, and neighboring high school. During the fourteen years that this center was open it became increasing apparent

to not only the homeless providers, but to the community at large how essential the NLEC Veterans Coming Home Center was. For that reason the Ozark Partnership and the City of Springfield not only encouraged New Life Evangelistic Center to expand it's hours of operation, but it also gave NLEC $5,000 a month for doing such. As a result, instead of closing at 3pm during the months of November through March, it remained open until 8 pm on nights the temperature was below 32° and 6 pm when the temperature was above 32°. In order to accomplish this expansion, the NLEC Veterans Coming Home Center had to expand its staff and transferred Mark Glenn from St. Louis to Springfield to help Chris Rice in his supervisory capacity.

Mark shared, "I came to the doors at NLEC at 16 where I was welcomed with loving arms by Larry and Penny Rice. They entered me into the training program, and I have been on FIRE for Jesus ever since! God summoned me in His loud voice and led me to NLEC through the ZOA Free Newspaper. If that had not happened, I do not know where I would be today!"

"Every time I returned to NLEC over the past 50 years, New Life Evangelistic Center has always welcomed me with open and loving arms. I am here to testify as the singer Andre Crouch sings in his song, 'Through it All', I have learned to trust in Jesus, I have learned to trust in God. He is faithful in accomplishing and completing his 50-year promise to me, His servant and to the NLEC ministry!"

In October Mike Humphreys who worked with Debra maintaining the 1411 Locust building went to the hospital with heart problems. He was to have a heart procedure done on Thursday, October 21st. When I had talked to Mike that previous Tuesday, he expressed it was going to be a routine treatment. That wasn't the case. As the treatment was taking place, Mike went into cardiac arrest for six to eight minutes. He never regained consciousness.

Daily I would go up to see Mike and would talk to him even though he was unconscious. The nurse attending him said it was good he could hear a familiar voice. These visits became increasingly difficult after Mike was taken off life support and became weaker with each passing day. On Thursday, November 4th at 4:28 pm Mike Humphries passed from this life into the next. Now he is with Jesus praising God with Scott, Penny, Mike Speaks, Jim Barnes, Slim and Zella Mae Cox and many other faithful members of the NLEC team who have gone on before us.

In the month of November, the Director of Missouri's State and Federal Surplus programs helped New Life Evangelistic Center acquire the items necessary for the homeless living outside. Stephanie, the Director of that agency searched not only for surplus items she could get in Missouri but also Texas, Nebraska, and Pennsylvania. As a result of her efforts NLEC received hundreds of sleeping bags, tents, socks and other items for as little as $1 a piece. These supplies would have cost New Life much more on the open market. Because of this

miracle, hundreds of homeless individuals were helped in their time of need.

The money saved on these emergency items allowed NLEC to directly help even more homeless individuals with their emergency needs. Those assisted included the 79-year-old man and a young lady who were sleeping under a tree in the park across from city hall. When the NLEC first responders to the homeless learned they were stranded travelers from Las Vegas, New Life acquired bus tickets so they could return home.

As the New Life Evangelistic Center team prepared to celebrate fifty years of God's faithfulness in 2022, we continued to witness His faithfulness the last two weeks of November. This demonstration of God's love was clearly seen through the miraculous provision of two unexpected gifts of $50,000. The fact was God's faithfulness went far beyond the paying of bills. It included His daily provision of dedicated staff and volunteers but even more importantly, the outpouring of the Holy Spirit during the daily trials, tribulations, and losses. The knowledge of the Resurrection of Jesus Christ would sustain and strengthen us so we could continue in the work God had given us.

During the month of December, I earnestly prayed that as New Life Evangelistic Center had its Christmas party outside of the 1411 Locust building, Jesus would provide a warm day. He answered that prayer with a December heat wave of 70°! On December 25th a great celebration of the birth of Jesus Christ took place which included a continental breakfast, followed by the distribution of $15 gift certificates to local restaurants, bus tickets and Bibles.

In addition, hygiene kits, sleeping bags, socks, gloves, earmuffs, hats, and bags of food were distributed to 250 homeless people. A Christmas free store of coats, warm clothes, kitchen items and toys was set up. This allowed that the homeless could not only get the additional items they needed but also gave them the opportunity to do last minute Christmas shopping for family and friends.

The Christmas Celebration that New Life Evangelistic Center had for the homeless involved not only the distribution of items to help them survive outside but included the provision of hope that only Christ can give. The Bibles, written Christmas message and the love flowing through the volunteers and NLEC staff all pointed to Jesus. Everyone attending was reminded that Jesus is the reason for the season.

New Life Evangelistic Center was now preparing to celebrate fifty years of following Jesus into the pain and suffering of the homeless and hurting. This involved working to meet the total needs of each hurting individual which included the physical mental and spiritual needs. As there needs were met those being assisted learned of the hope and help Jesus provides both now and for all eternity.

Chapter 12
Continuing to Follow Jesus into the Suffering of the Homeless

Maria & Shawn

As the New Life Evangelistic Center staff followed Jesus into the pain of the homeless, they met Marie and her son Shawn. This mother and her 5-year-old son were living in a tent before coming to New Life. Marie shared, "I didn't know how I would find the help that I needed, except to pray. God answered my prayer when another homeless person found the book I had lost with NLEC's address in it and returned the book to me! I immediately came to New Life Evangelistic Center with my son and found a new home and family that day!

New Life Evangelistic Center for fifty years has followed Jesus into the suffering of the poor and homeless. There it has built relationships

and witnessed how all human beings are created in the image of God and in need of a place they can feel at home. It believes, as the Scripture says, that "God places the lonely in families" (Psalm 68:6).

This family is the New Life Evangelistic Center Community where individuals are challenged to live out their God given calling or purpose. NLEC by its very efforts to provide a home within the Biblical context is considered a threat to the shallow government claims of ending chronic homelessness by placing a few in shelter without purpose and the reality of the presence of God.

This need for purpose is illustrated by the life of Gary, a former Vietnam War Veteran. Gary was in his early forties when he came to the New Life Evangelistic Center. He was a homeless man who was tired of searching for a place he could call home. When he came to the doors of NLEC for the first time he thought he was coming to a place where he would only find shelter. What he found was an opportunity to become a part of the New Life family and a place to call home.

Gary's new home was a place of residence, a resting place, a place to create memories, a place of hospitality, a place for order, acceptance, and a sense of belonging. As a leader at NLEC's New Bloomfield renewable energy center Gary not only lived with a sense of purpose, but he transferred that to other previously homeless people as well. Most importantly of all Gary had allowed himself to be awakened to the power and presence of God.

In his new home Gary had learned not only how to live but also to die. As Gary neared his fiftieth birthday his heart began to fail him to the point his doctor and nurse encouraged him to move into hospice. But Gary had found his home and did not want to leave. He continued to work in the NLEC renewable energy center as long as he could. Then when he could no longer work the men took turns caring for him in his bedroom.

Gary had discovered the power of prayer, faith, compassion, relationships and hope in his new home at NLEC. As he faced death Gary knew he was simply getting ready for his eternal home. He had spent his life being uprooted and then rooted at New Life Evangelistic Center. Now he was traveling to his eternal home where death, mourning and crying will be no more.

After being blown over, homeless Gary had been replanted in the love of Christ. Behind New Life Evangelistic Center new headquarters at 2428 Woodson Road in Overland five years ago a large oak tree blew over. It laid there on its side, uprooted with its roots still intact. After being cut off about 8 feet above the ground, this tree was pulled upright and left that way.

As time passed that tree started to sprout again as described in Job 14:7 where it says, "At least there is hope for a tree: If it is cut down, it will sprout again, and its new sprouts will not fail."

Now as the NLEC staff and those in its residential training program go out to the parking lot each day, they see this tree which has a new beginning. They are then reminded that in spite of their past they also can, through the love of Christ, start all over again.

During the past fifty years New Life Evangelistic Center has continued to stand firm in spite of the winds of adversity that have blown against it. When blown over and seemingly uprooted by the closing of 1411 Locust, the Holy Spirit has re-established this work so it could continue to sprout for the glory of God.

With the arrival of 2022, New Life Evangelistic Center entered into its fiftieth year of service. In spite of the trials and tribulations it had faced, for the first time in three years, New Life closed 2021 with all the bills of the previous year paid. In addition, New Life Evangelistic Center on January 2, 2022, received word that the City of St. Louis had accepted NLEC's architectural plans for 1411 Locust. This miraculously opened the door for New Life to work to get an occupancy permit to reopen 1411 Locust as a day facility for the homeless. In addition, God had continued to heal Jeff Schneider until he was able to direct the construction team to make the necessary renovations.

As New Life Evangelistic Center celebrated God's faithfulness during the past fifty years, we joyfully looked with anticipation for the Holy Spirit to lead us into the future. Christ has planted a vision in the heart of the New Life Evangelistic Center staff and partners to move forward for the glory of God. We have witnessed God's faithfulness and continued to believe Him to do exceedingly above what we could ask or think through Christ Jesus who strengthened us (Ephesians 3:20).

On January 22, 2022, New Life Evangelistic Center celebrated its Fiftieth Anniversary with over one hundred and seventy-five faithful partners at a celebration banquet at the Orlando's Banquet Center. My son Chris who directs NLEC's ministry in the Marshfield, Springfield, and Joplin area presented a dynamic video giving an overview of the past 50 years of New Life Evangelistic Center's ministry.

During the banquet Chris Aaron my grandson shared, "A quick glance at the history of New Life exposes the spirit of innovation and vision. We were the first to give out fans and car seats to the elderly and poor. NLEC was the first to create the Winter Patrol and train the homeless in radio and television broadcasting. The list goes on and on. The point is, NLEC seeks to find the needs that aren't being filled than under the Holy Spirit's direction works to meet these needs. I am committed to help lead New Life Evangelistic Center into more firsts."

In the weeks that followed Chris Aaron went into further detail describing the need for opening a day center in St. Louis. "In the sweltering heat or frigid cold, there is little hope for rest without a place to go. How can we expect men and women to take the necessary steps to break the cycle of homelessness, when they are constantly moved from place to place? With no low barrier day center, the unhoused community scatters across the city. This makes it nearly impossible for caseworkers to meet with and assist their clients in breaking the cycle of homelessness. Access to basic health needs such as, clean water, bathrooms, hygiene items and first aid are limited or non-existent on the streets. The homeless often feel rejected, hurt and alone. Every human being deserves the basic necessities of life and not forced to be alone in the parks."

The vision for New Life Evangelistic Center didn't just include a day center but also a large overnight walk-in shelter in St. Louis County where none exists. Chris Aaron went into further explain of this vision, "I envision New Life opening the first low barrier, easily accessible emergency shelter in St Louis County. By working alongside St Louis County, we will begin to make a real difference for men and women on the streets. As it is right now, there is no walk-in shelters for men and women to go in St. Louis County. The homeless are left to fend for themselves or forced to go to the city where unfamiliarity and danger lurks. I am committed to helping lead the charge for change in St. Louis County."

On February 24, 2022 Russia invaded the Ukraine. This invasion created Europe's largest refugee crisis since World War II. The invasion was widely condemned internationally as an act of aggression with many countries imposing new sanctions on Russia.

As women, children and the elderly fled the country, martial law was imposed. All male Ukrainian men between the ages of 16 and 60 years of age were not allowed to leave Ukraine and were conscripted for military service.

In April, Chris Aaron shared the following with our NLEC partners, "Ukraine is very close to my heart. I have been to this beautiful country 3 times. My wife, Irene, is Ukrainian and all my in-laws are still there. Recently, God has laid a vision on my heart and that of my grandfather, Larry Rice to assist the people of Ukraine. We must not only help the refugees coming to America, but we also must seek God as to how we can help refuges in Ukraine. Many who have fled their homes in the Eastern part of Ukraine have gone to Western Ukraine where they are now in need of help."

Chris Aaron's goes on to say, "As NLEC helps those in need in Ukraine it continues and will continue to help each homeless and hurting person who comes to New Life Evangelistic Center." This proves to be true by testimonies of those who are receiving help daily at NLEC.

Audrey and her children ended up homeless after her house burned down. She had nowhere to go and through a series of miracles came to one of the NLEC Safe Houses. For over two years Audrey stayed at the Safe House until she got a job and with NLEC's assistance a house for her and her four children.

Audrey with three of her children

Michelle testified, "I have been through abuse that I have never experienced before, mentally, physically, and financially. My family was too far away to help and so I found myself needing to go and find a city that had the resources I needed. I overshot my bus stop and ended up homeless in St. Louis. There, a homeless man came up and talked to me. He saw I was cold, hungry, hurting and exhausted. He referred me to Pastor Ray, who in turn drove me to the NLEC Administration and Training Center to enter one of the Safe Houses. There I received the help I needed."

"I was given something to eat and a warm bed to sleep in and a shower, which felt better than anything on earth at that moment. I actually wanted to cry that NLEC and everyone else involved helped me. For the first time in a long time I felt like I wasn't drowning."

Alyssa & Noah

Alyssa wrote, "I am so grateful for New Life Evangelistic Center! Without the safe haven I have found at the Safe House, Noah and I would be out on the streets with nowhere to go! Now, I can focus on working and saving the money needed provide a home of our own."

Karen came to New Life Evangelistic Center after her life fell apart. She says, "I am so blessed to have found a family and a renewed hope for my life through the staff at New Life Evangelistic Center. I now have the opportunity to heal from my past and build a new future with Jesus Christ knowing that he will never leave me or forsake me."

New Life Evangelistic Center has been able to follow Jesus for fifty years into the pain of the hurting and homeless because of its caring partners. The faithful prayers and gifts of these compassion individuals have made it possible for the NLEC staff to provide hope to those who were unable to find help anywhere else.

In the midst of pain of the hurting and homeless the staff found daily strength in scriptures like Hebrews 10:23 which says, "Let us hold unswervingly to the hope we profess, for He who promised is faithful".

It is this hope that fueled the staff of New Life Evangelistic Center to double their efforts to be "hope dealers" on the street once 1411 Locust was closed. It involved not only expanding present NLEC programs but involved a team daily providing hope to those who were homeless.

Karen

New Life became the number one provider of transportation assistance for the homeless with the distribution of over 1,000 bus tickets weekly. Additional Safe Houses were opened for the homeless women and children as the training programs were expanded for the homeless men.

Homeless individuals are not only being helped in the greater St. Louis area but also at New Life's Veterans Coming Home Center at 806 N. Jefferson in Springfield, Missouri. Michael writes, "I have burned down all the bridges in my life. I am so glad the New Life Veterans Coming Home Center threw me out a lifeline of hope and help. It is more than a place for food and clothes, but a place where I can mediate on God and my present journey."

Michael

Tyrone shares how Jesus set him free to work at the NLEC Veterans Coming Home Center in Springfield, MO. ""I was a troubled man. My life was a struggle. As my drinking alcohol increased my life became more chaotic. I needed help! A friend told me about the New Life Training Program. So, I gave up everything I had

Tyrone assisting client at the VCHC Center in Springfield, MO

146

including myself and joined the program. I was sent to New Bloom-field where I found peace and more Jesus. We had morning devo-tionals and tasks to be completed every day. I discovered God's way was better than my way. I am in Springfield now where my training continues. I now help out the center in checking in clients and advis-ing them of our services. I am doing things now which I thought was impossible! Thank you, New Life and Jesus!"

Roxy said, "I was addicted to Satan's meth for years. I wound up in jail, and found Jesus! Even though I was incarcerated, I praised the Lord every day! I read His Word. I cried out to the Lord in prayer! I became addicted to Jesus rather than meth! I have been clean now for 80 days! The New Life VCHC is a great place to get meals and new clothes and inspirational devotions as I rebuild my life. I am liv-

Roxy

ing proof that Jesus has come to 'set the cap-tives free'"!

Kevin shares, "I got COVID. It viciously at-tacked my body and forced me into the hos-pital. Things got worse when the doctors dis-covered the left side of my heart was enlarged. I knew I was near death. I could feel my heart pounding in my chest. I sat on the edge of the hospital bed and said, "God save me, please! I want to live for my friends and my family. I want to live for YOU!" I felt a peace wash over me. He saved me! While spending time at the New Life VCHC, I am applying for places to stay, and I tell others about the goodness of God. To God be the glory for

Kevin

the great things He has done in sav-ing a wretch like me!"

Like Michael, Roxy and Kevin, I knew how critical it is to meditate on the goodness and glory of God as I travel the journey of life. It is for that reason that I daily go on "prayer walks" ob-serving the wonders of God's creation.

As the year 2022 progressed I took the lessons I had learned from this daily journey in God's creation and wrote a sixteen-chapter book. The title of the book which is available on Amazon is "Creation Care Moments."

In Chapter 7 I wrote, "All of us sooner or later find ourselves in dirty places. At moments like that everything can appear dark and lonely. It is then we must ask the Holy Spirit to show us in the natural realm what is also seen in the spiritual world. This is because both are woven together. In John 12:24 Jesus says, "Most assuredly, I say to you, unless a grain of wheat falls into the ground and dies, it remains along: but if it dies, it produces much grain."

"The fact is it is hard being a seed in the ground. It is lonely there and dark. Yet Jesus said unless we like seeds are not buried in what seems like dirty places, we can't produce much fruit or grain."

"The challenge is how we, like seeds, germinate in those lonely dirty places. When we find ourselves like seeds buried in dirty places, we feel lost in loneliness. When that happens, we must remember we are not alone. Christ is with us, and He has also sent the Comforter, the Holy Spirit, and the angels to directly assist us as they convert those dirty places into good nourishing soil."

"In the midst of the dirty places, we must take seriously our angelic inheritance described in verses like Psalm 91:9-12 where it says, "If you make the Most High your dwelling – even the Lord, who is my refuge – then no harm will befall you, no disaster will come near your tent. For He will command His angels concerning you to guard you in all your ways; they will life you up in their hands, so that you will not strike your foot against a stone."

Seth shares his experience of being buried in a dark dirty place and the germination that took place. "I took a cocktail of many drugs and blacked out behind my steering wheel. Amazingly, I did not total my car, or kill someone! I don't even remember being in my car... I just remember my soul being in darkness. Like a darkness you can feel. I was dying, suffocating as this blackness filled my lungs. Then a light came and rose my soul out of the darkness! It was Jesus! I was alive! I opened my eyes and I was in a hospital bed with doctors shocking my heart back to life! I praise the Lord every day for my second chance! I am using the resources at the New Life VCHC to get my life back on track!"

William shares how he was living homeless under a bridge until Jesus set him free to serve Him at the NLEC Veterans Coming Home Center in Springfield, MO. "After the loss of my family and my twin brother, I became homeless. I was sleeping under a bridge when Rev. Ray found me. I was dirty, hungry, alone, and afraid. It was through the NLEC Training Program in New Bloomfield where I finally found my security. I discovered security through the program and Jesus

William giving client mail at the front desk in Springfield, MO

Christ. I now work in Springfield helping with the mail and other front desk duties. For sure my life is 1,000 times better as I can now not only help others but tell them Jesus saves!"

Daily the NLEC Staff have a multitude of opportunities to let the love of God shine through them because of the caring partners who support NLEC. The love of Christ is shown daily through the work of New Life Evangelistic Center in so many ways. Lee saw it when he was provided a new tire.

"I haven't been able to get my life together since my wife died. Lost our home in my grief and made my car my new home. I wind up spending most of my disability check on keeping this put-put a puttering. Now I need help! I came to the New Life VCHC for assistance in getting me a new tire for my car/home. I know they don't typically help with car repairs, so I want to thank them for being there when I needed them! Thanks for the tire! Thanks for showing me the love of Jesus!"

As the temperature started to soar in the month of May New Life Evangelistic Center expanded its efforts to get water into the hands of homeless who urgently needed such.

Sleepy, a homeless man, who lost his leg through a car accident says, "On these hot summer days, water is vital to me staying alive."

Debbie explains, "It gets hot our here! I need water to live, to take my medicine, to cool off my body, to quench my thirst. A bottle of cold water just touches my whole being."

Joe is a Desert Storm Veteran who says, "water is not an option. We must have it to live! As a homeless veteran finding fresh, clean water is hard. Many businesses won't even give me a cup of water!"

Sleepy

Bernard says, "Water is vital and there are few places to get what is supposed to be free! I am homeless due to an eviction, but even without a home I can count on New Life Evangelistic Center to get food, cloth-

149

ing, and lifesaving water!"

While the NLEC first responders among the homeless were on the front lines helping thirsty, hungry, and hurting people through out Mid America, Chris Aaron his wife Irene and daughter Abby were in Ukraine. They left June 11th and returned late June 29th.

Joe

Bernard

While they were in Ukraine Chris Aaron and Irene worked closely with churches in various areas of Western Ukraine. From the relationships born during that visit the following vision came forth in Chris Aaron's life.

"Since the beginning of this war, millions of children in Ukraine have been displaced. Every day they fear the next missile strike will kill them or their loved ones. The physical and mental harm done by Russia's terror lasts much longer than the air sirens. The nights are spent listening to these air sirens, bombs dropping and seeing friends and family mercilessly killed."

"In the midst of all this pain, God is working for His perfect pleasure. Many men and women are coming to a saving faith in Jesus Christ as their Lord and Savior. I have personally heard testimonies of growing faith in God in the midst of suffering. New Life Evangelistic Center is following Jesus into the hurt and pain of Ukrainians. NLEC Is committed to working with local churches in Ukraine to minister to hurting people during this war."

Irene working in a Free Store for Refugees

"The dreams of the children of Ukraine have turned into nightmares. This daily trauma has stopped their hopes for the future. These are dreams that pull life forward which have been crushed along with the hopes for life and peace."

"New Life Evangelistic Center envisions building a community of hope and restoration in Ukraine. By working alongside local churches in Ukraine that NLEC has built relationships with."

"The hope these children have for tomorrow lies in the heads, hearts, and hands of people of faith. God has entrusted us with the opportuni- ty for Ukrainian children to see His love in action, working through His people of compassion. We can build them new homes, new hopes, and new opportuni- ties. The power of the Holy Spirit work- ing through the people of God is great- er than Putin's bombs. It is this power that will build a future for the children of Ukraine."

"The NLEC City of Refuge will have a resource center for other mem- bers in the community. This community center will help refugees find housing, employ- ment, counseling, and other neces- sary resources in Lutsk. Current- ly there are no centers like this where a variety of resources can be

Children playing in Ukraine

found in one location. This resource center would also operate as a church serving the city of refuge as their central place of worship."

While Chris Aaron and Irene were in Ukraine trying to help the home- less refugees there, Ray, Joe, Glen and myself were working through- out Mid-America to help the homeless here. The numbers of those of homeless people who were living outside in the greater St. Louis area were growing in numbers due to punitive legislation by local and state officials. In May St. Louis city leaders passed legislation making it a crime for homeless individuals to sleep anywhere on city property.

In June the governor of the state of Missouri signed HB 1606 into law. After slowly studying this law that Chris, my son, had brought to my attention, I wrote the following.

"This law clearly states that if any political subdivision has a higher per capita rate of homelessness than the state average, such political subdivision will, "within one year of the passage of this act, receive no further state funding by the department."

"As ridiculous as it is to lock up the homeless at a cost to tax payers of up to a $100 a day, the provisions of HB 1606 is even more dangerous when it says that if political subdivisions do not aggressively deal with the homeless with the inhuman methods laid out in this draconian law, 'the attorney general shall have the power to bring a civil action in any court of competent jurisdiction against any political subdivision to enjoin the political subdivision from violating the provision of this subsection.' Section 5. (5) of HB 1606 goes on to say, 'the attorney general may recover reasonable expenses incurred in any civil action brought under this section, including court costs, reasonable attorney fees, investigative costs, witness fees and deportation costs.'"

"John who lost his leg due to diabetes because he did not get medical attention, lives under the Loughborough highway 55 overpass. He is just one of many who are being pushed out of their encampments due to this state law."

"Never in fifty years of working to assist the homeless in the state of Missouri have I seen such an oppressive law as HB 1606. Not only does it further criminalize the homeless but also those communities in which the homeless struggle to survive within."

"HB 1606 in section 7 says, 'Any political subdivision with a higher per-capita rate of homelessness than the state average, as determined by the most recent United States Census numbers.... And point-in-time continuum of care count... within one year of the passage of this act, receive no further state funding.'"

After writing this I continued to see how the war on poverty had become the war on the impoverished. The ongoing blaming and criminalizing of the homeless is so far removed from the teachings of Jesus who said, "As often as you have done it to the least of these, even so you have done it unto me".

Some of the first victims of HB 1606 were John and Julia. John who had lost his leg due to diabetes lived in his wheelchair under the Loughborough Highway 55 overpass. After John and the homeless were forced out of their home under the overpass they scattered throughout the area. Later, the New Life first responders found John living in a nearby park.

Twenty-eight-year-old Julie also resided under the same overpass where a dozen other homeless individuals lived. Julie was five months pregnant. After giving her immediate assistance, I invited Julie to one of the New Life Evangelistic Center Safe Houses. Before I could return to further assist her and the homeless in that community, they had been driven from that location and all their possessions removed.

New Life Evangelistic Center continues to follow Jesus into the suffering of the homeless wherever they may be. Not only do we find these hurting men, woman and children throughout Mid-America but around the world in locations like Ukraine, India, Haiti and Africa.

Charles shares how he was found in his time of need. "I gotta be honest. My addiction to meth caused me to be homeless. Living on the streets is like living in pure hell. Recently someone stole everything I had. Clothes, backpack and my tent. Glad to be able to get help from the New Life VCHC. They gave me new clothes, hygiene kits, food and a new tent! I use the center as a place to look for a job and to keep me sober. Please pray for me and others who want to break the chains of addiction and homelessness."

Jesus not only calls us to follow Him and share His love among the hurting and the homeless, but He equips us through the power of the Holy Spirit. In Deuteronomy 31:8 we are told that as we face the challenges of the future, "The Lord Himself goes before you and will be with you, He will never leave you nor forsake you. Do not be afraid; do not be discouraged."

Romans 8:37 further tells us that, "We are more than conquerors through Christ, who loved us."

After 50 years of following Jesus into a suffering world, the New Life Evangelistic Center team can face the uncertainty of the future with the knowledge God is with us. It is a fact we are more than conquerors through Christ who loves us.

Larry writes about how Jesus made him more than a conqueror by taking him from homelessness to Godliness. "I began my renewed Christian journey in New Bloomfield. I loved the intense Bible Studies and prayer. My life was saved! From homelessness to Godliness! Now I work in the kitchen in Springfield at the New Life VCHC. I am learning so much about God and discipline."

The world and its needs have radically changed during the past fifty years, but Chris Aaron and the new generation of partners accompanying him can know that "Jesus Christ is the same yesterday, today and forever" (Hebrews 13:8).

With that knowledge we can be certain that, "He who has begun a good work in you will bring it to completion at the day of Jesus Christ" (Philippians 1:6).

Epilogue

As 2022 came to conclusion, Charlie Hale, who had been working for New Life Evangelistic Center for over twenty-three years, gave his notice of resignation. Charlie was secretary on the NLEC Board of Directors and New Life's Chief Financial Officer. Since he had given thirty-days' notice, this gave Charlie the opportunity to teach Chris Aaron all aspects of his day-to-day activities and for Chris Aaron to replace him on the New Life Evangelistic Center Board of Directors as Secretary. Through this position of overseeing the NLEC IT, Media, Financial and Legal Departments, Chris Aaron would gain invaluable experience for someday directing the growing ministry of New Life Evangelistic Center.

Although I know I will always have a place at NLEC, I do know God is doing a great and mighty work through Chris Aaron's leadership. This new work will allow New Life Evangelistic Center to share hope and help through the love of Jesus Christ with many more individuals in need around the world. As this happens, the prayers and financial support of the New Life partners will become increasingly valuable in the years to come.

How I thank God for these precious individuals who have made it possible for NLEC to share for over fifty years in word and deed that there is hope because Chris is Risen.

Our primary prayer as we move into the future must be "Father God, please in the name of Jesus, send the Holy Spirit". With St. Louis now being named the most dangerous city in America, this prayer is more urgent than ever before.

New Life Evangelistic Center was born in the middle of such a movement in 1972 (See AJ Medlock's article from the State Historical Society in Chapter 2). This movement of the Holy Spirit was known then as the Jesus Movement or the Charismatic Movement. At that time thousands upon thousands of individuals, hungry for spiritual, political, and social change would seek God for an outpouring of the Holy Spirit that would bring them closer to Jesus.

I can understand the skepticism of those who upon looking at the violence, political polarization, and mass human needs today, believe

such a movement of the Holy Spirit is not possible. The reason I know that not only is such a movement of God possible because I have been in such, but also and most importantly of all the Bible tells me that such can and will take place. (2 Chronicles 7:14, Joel 2:28-29, 2 Corinthians 5:17).

The symbol of New Life Evangelistic Center during these past 50 years has been the arch, the cross, and the dove symbolizing the Holy Spirit. It is the Holy Spirit pouring out the love of Christ upon not only St. Louis but at this critical moment in our countries history that is so urgently needed. When this happens, not only will the hungry be fed and the homeless housed, but we will become a community of people where the world will know that we are Christians by our love.

Find us on Social Media

TWITTER.COM/NewLifeSTL
FACEBOOK.COM/NewLife STL
YOUTUBE.COM/NewLifeEvangCenter
INSTAGRAM.COM/NewLifeSTL

NLEC TV

Available in App Stores

NLEC TV'S
CREATION CARE MESSAGES

Watch NLEC TV's Creation Care Messages anytime, anywhere! Visit the NLEC TV app or website to view the live stream of our programming.

1.

Visit the NLEC TV app or website
Download the NLEC TV app from your preferred app store (iTunes, Google Play, Amazon, etc).

2.

Watch/Listen

Watch or Listen
Open the NLEC TV app and click on the Watch/Listen tab at the bottom of the screen.

3.

Creation Cares Messages
Click on the Creation Cares Messages Live Stream graphic.

4.

Creation Care Messages Live Stream

Play the Live Stream
Click the play button on the screen that opens.

New Life Evangelistic Center
2428 Woodson Rd., Overland, MO 63114
Phone 314-421-3020
Veterans Coming Home Center
806 N. Jefferson Ave., Springfield, MO
65802
Phone 417-866-3363